An Inv...

In 2001 it will be ten years since BR... 1997, a Service of Thanksgiving and... London, marked our 75th anniversa... of Celebration and Thanksgiving, an... Vice Presidents will be our preachers...

SATURDAY 12 MAY 2001

St Helen's Parish Church, Wirral, Merseyside at 2.00pm
Preacher: The Rt Revd Dr James Jones, Bishop of Liverpool

SATURDAY 9 JUNE 2001

Christchurch, Clifton, Bristol at 2.00pm
Preacher: The Revd Baroness Richardson of Calow OBE

SATURDAY 22 SEPTEMBER 2001

Durham Cathedral at 2.00pm
Preacher: The Rt Revd Michael Turnbull, Bishop of Durham

SATURDAY 27 OCTOBER 2001

Bury St Edmunds Cathedral at 2.00pm
*Preacher: The Revd Canon Dr Christina Baxter, Principal,
St John's Nottingham*

❖

These services will provide an opportunity for all of us involved with BRF in whatever way—readers, subscribers, supporters, authors, contributors to the Bible reading notes, trustees and staff—to celebrate and give thanks for all that has taken place within BRF over the past decade.

We hope very much that many of you, the readers of our Bible reading notes, will be able to join us on one (or more) of these important occasions, and we extend a very warm invitation to you all.

Admission to the services will be by ticket, and you are welcome to apply for as many tickets as you would like. If you wish to bring friends or are able to bring a group from your church, we would be delighted.
Please complete the form overleaf to apply for tickets.

(PLEASE PRINT)

Name:_____

Address:_____

_____

_____ Postcode: _____

Telephone (day): _____

Telephone (evening): _____

E-mail: _____

Please send me tickets for the following service(s):

Qty

☐ Saturday 12 May 2001, St Helen's Parish Church, 2.00pm   _____

☐ Saturday 9 June 2001, Christchurch, Clifton, Bristol, 2.00pm   _____

☐ Saturday 22 Sept 2001, Durham Cathedral, 2.00pm   _____

☐ Saturday 27 Oct 2001, Bury St Edmunds Cathedral, 2.00pm   _____

Total number of tickets: _____

Please send your completed form to:

2001 Service Ticket Dept
BRF
Peter's Way
Sandy Lane West
Oxford
OX4 6HG

Ticket applications will be processed strictly on a first-come, first-served basis. We will advise you if your application arrives after all the tickets have been allocated. If you do not hear from us, you may assume that tickets have been reserved for you as requested, and these will be despatched approximately three weeks before each service takes place.

JANUARY–APRIL 2001

Guidelines

VOLUME 17 / PART 1

Edited by **Grace Emmerson and John Parr**

The Bible Reading Fellowship
OPENING THE BIBLE

Writers in this issue

Romans   **John Proctor** works for the United Reformed Church as New Testament lecturer at Westminster College, Cambridge. He studied for church ministry at Glasgow University and served at a Church of Scotland parish in Glasgow from 1981 to 1986..

On growing old   **John Eaton**, formerly Reader in Old Testament Studies in the University of Birmingham, has published several works on Old Testament subjects, including *The Circle of Creation: Animals in the Light of the Bible* (SCM Press).

Judges 9—16   **Stephen Dawes** is Chairman of the Cornwall District of the Methodist Church. Formerly he taught Old Testament and Hebrew at Trinity College, Legon, Ghana and at Queen's College, Birmingham. He is the author of the volume on 1 and 2 Kings for the BRF commentary series, *The People's Bible Commentary*.

The Sunday of Forgiveness   **Robert Atwell** is Vicar of St Mary's, Primrose Hill, in north London. He was previously Chaplain of Trinity College, Cambridge, where he taught Patristics, and for ten years a Benedictine monk in a monastery in the Cotswolds. He is editor of two collections of daily readings for use with the Church of England Calendar: *Celebrating the Saints* and *Celebrating the Seasons* (Canterbury Press, 1998, 1999).

Ecclesiastes   **John Goldingay** teaches Old Testament at Fuller Theological Seminary in Pasadena, California. He watches films, goes to jazz clubs, sits in the sun, drinks wine, writes books on the Old Testament, looks after his disabled wife, Ann, and thinks of England, but not very wistfully.

The Gospel of Matthew   **Elizabeth Raine** is a minister of the Word in the Uniting Church in Australia, and works for the Board of Social Responsibility in Sydney. She has worked in education, health care, student chaplaincy and theological education. She is currently completing her doctoral research on the Gospel of Matthew for the University of Durham.

Hosea   **Michael Tunnicliffe** is a Methodist minister living in Warrington. He is the author of *Chronicles to Nehemiah* in the BRF *People's Bible Commentary* series.

THE GUIDELINES
Magazine

The BRF Prayer

O God our Father,
in the holy scriptures
you have given us your word
to be our teacher and guide:
help us and all the members of our Fellowship
to seek in our reading
the guidance of the Holy Spirit
that we may learn more of you
and of your will for us,
and so grow in likeness to your Son,
Jesus Christ our Lord.
Amen.

Editors' Letter

A happy new year—some might want to say 'a happy new millennium'—to all *Guidelines* readers. We begin this issue with Paul's letter to the Romans. The notes are written by a regular contributor, John Proctor, who underlines the concern for mission that informs this magisterial statement of the apostle's gospel. At the request of one of our readers, we include a week's notes on the topic of 'Growing Old'. Be assured, their interest is not restricted to the elderly! Writing with all our readers in mind, John Eaton, another regular contributor, invites us to share his personal reflections and warm memories of sometimes eccentric characters. Full of faith and hope, we trust that they will bring encouragement to many.

In today's violent and manipulative world, the tales of deception and intrigue in Judges 9—16 (among them the love story of Samson and Delilah) take on fresh interest. Stephen Dawes' notes are both informative and challenging. A new contributor, Robert Atwell, takes us into Lent. The title of his notes comes from the Eastern Orthodox Church's designation of the Sunday before Lent as the Sunday of Forgiveness. His readings from Genesis explore the themes of forgiveness and reconciliation in these well-known stories. John Goldingay writes from the USA on the ancient musings on life found in Ecclesiastes. Although this book raises more questions than it provides answers, it compels us to face our self-deception in today's frenetic society. Drawing on his own experience of sadness, John writes with sensitivity, aware of what it means to wrestle with hard questions. 'Against the background of the fact of death, Ecclesiastes invites his audience to affirm life.'

Elizabeth Raine's notes on the final part of Matthew's Gospel lead us through the rest of Lent and into Holy Week and Easter. We are reminded of the way the Gospels can be used to fuel anti-Jewish sentiments when they are read carelessly. And we also see the implications for mission in the way Matthew tells the Easter story. After Easter we are in the company of Hosea, with his powerful message of God's unwearied love in the face of rejection, and his warnings of disaster for those who 'sow the wind and reap the whirlwind'. Michael Tunnicliffe brings the prophet's word to bear on today's social ills and political instability.

Your letters remind us of our privilege as editors in helping to make possible a series of conversations. The most obvious one is between *Guidelines* readers and contributors. But the most important one is between Bible readers and God. We hope that these conversations will continue to encourage all of us to think and pray and live more faithfully in the way of Jesus Christ.

Grace Emmerson, John Parr (Guidelines Editors)

Christians in the Armed Forces

Alexine Crawford

There was a time when, on the strength of what seemed to me to be key verses, I considered that for a Christian to be in the armed forces was wrong. 'Thou shalt not kill' is the sixth commandment (Exodus 20); Jesus said, 'Those who draw the sword will die by the sword' (Matthew 26:52); Peter wrote, 'Do not repay evil with evil' (1 Peter 3:9), and Jesus said, 'Do not resist one who is evil. But if anyone strikes you on the right cheek, turn to him the other also' (Matthew 5:39).

Yet the Old Testament is full of wars and fighting, often with God actively involved. And for each of those 'key' verses I discovered others that seemed to run counter to them. After the last supper, for instance, with crisis imminent, Jesus said, 'If you don't have a sword, sell your cloak and buy one.' This sounds like a sanction to defend themselves, yet he told them off when one of them did (Luke 22:36, 38).

Later that same night, the high priest was endeavouring to get Jesus to condemn himself out of his own mouth. When Jesus objected to their illegal procedure, one of the officers nearby hit him across the face. So Jesus offered his other cheek for the officer to hit? Not at all. He said, 'If I have spoken wrongly, bear witness to the wrong; but if I have spoken rightly, why do you strike me?' (John 18:22–23).

Peace in the vast Roman Empire was maintained by its armies, so, to the writers of the New Testament, a military presence guarding law and order was part of everyday life. Paul was rescued by

The Old Testament is full of wars and fighting

soldiers from an angry mob, and sent to safety with a heavy military escort (Acts 21 and 23).

Soldiers crop up in the Gospels too, and nowhere are they condemned for being soldiers. John the Baptist baptized some. He did not tell them to resign, but simply told them to act justly and avoid violence. In the Gospels, the profession of arms excites no more comment than that of a fisherman.

So, I had to ask myself, is it all a muddle? Does scripture contradict itself? Then I married a soldier and encountered military life at first hand. We met with good Christian fellowship, and I began to see that I needed to look beyond isolated verses to a broader sweep of biblical truth. Isaiah (2:4) gives a beautiful picture of 'the latter days' when 'they will beat their swords into ploughshares, and their spears into pruning hooks; nation will not take up sword against nation, nor will they train for war any more.' Anyone who has suffered personally through war must especially long for that time. But attached to the promise, there is a condition. Before any possibility of its fulfilment, nations and peoples must yearn for God, saying, 'Come, let us go up to the mountain of the Lord… that he may teach us his ways and

What worries most people is the question of killing

that we may walk in his paths' (Isaiah 2:3).

We are not there yet. In a fallen world, human rule has to be based on a degree of force, from the discipline imposed by parents on a child to the punishment of wrongdoers and, if need be, to the use of arms in war. There has to be a profession of arms—today a navy and an air force as well as an army. I suppose, what most worries people is the question of killing, and how a Christian faces up to this.

Many of us live in a society where death has ceased to be an accepted fact of life. Although constantly depicted on television, actual death is hidden in hospitals and abattoirs. Its very remoteness from our normal experience lends it horror and dread. But God it seems has a different view of death. An incident in Acts 12 particularly struck me. King Herod had Peter arrested—Peter who had become prominent and bold in speaking about Jesus. This important prisoner was guarded by sixteen soldiers. At night he was handcuffed between two soldiers, and two others guarded the doors. And then an angel came, telling him to get up, get dressed and follow him into the city. In the morning, two horrified guards found empty handcuffs attached to their wrists and no one had seen anyone go out through the doors. Herod questioned the guards—and then had them put to death. Now God clearly knew that the penalty for soldiers on guard who let a prisoner escape would be death. Yet he miraculously rescued Peter and allowed those guards to be killed—a different perspective.

That sixth commandment is more accurately rendered 'You shall not murder'. The Bible distinguishes between war and violence. God sent war against Israel when the people persistently turned away from him, but the manner in which that war was carried out was the responsibility of the combatants. When God sent Assyria against Israel, he called it 'the rod of my anger, the staff of my fury', but the arrogant, destructive Assyrians went far beyond God's intention for them. Violence took over. Being authorized to take life is a tremendous responsibility, and it is vital to distinguish between killing and murder, to learn to eliminate any element of personal revenge. This is one aspect of training.

Constant training prepares members of the Forces not only to use their weapons efficiently and with restraint, but also to respond appropriately when they are tense or frightened or tired or angry.

It is vital to eliminate any element of personal revenge

Every kind of combat has to be practised so that it becomes almost instinctive, so that in a critical situation there is no 'shall I, shan't I' but a rehearsed series of questions leading to unhesitating action. This applies as much to the soldier on patrol in Ireland or Kosovo as to the airman flying in formation at tremendous speed. Their obligation is to be effective without violence. Christians have the added obligation to prepare themselves spiritually, and they have the immense advantage of prayer. People involved in recent conflicts have told me how they prayed constantly for safety, prayed for their fellows, prayed for their target that no one would unnecessarily be hit, prayed for prisoners rather than casualties. Christians also need to be sure enough and bold enough, if need arise, to stand their ground on moral issues.

During the Bosnia campaign in 1994–95, one of the Air Force commanders was a Christian. On several occasions he rejected the Air Tasking Orders given him. In his opinion, the bombs to be dropped, accurate though aiming has become, could not in the prevailing conditions be guaranteed to hit only the given military targets without damaging anything else nearby.

Because he had earned respect as an airman, the task was called off.

That action cannot have come easily to him, for service men and women are trained in obedience. Jesus commended the centurion who sent a message begging him to heal his servant—commended him because he understood obedience and the chain of command. The centurion expected to obey those in authority over him, and he expected those below him, for whom he held responsibility, to obey him (Luke 7:1–10).

Obedience and authority are unpopular in contemporary society, and since human beings are essentially rebellious, obedience is hard for us. As an Army wife I grappled with this, with my husband's ethos of obedience and with the regular house-moves that obedience demanded of us as a family. Yet God, over and over again, asks us to obey him and obey his precepts. Furthermore, both Paul in Romans 13 and Peter (1 Peter 2:13–14) urge us to obey and be subject to secular authority. Jesus told his hearers to 'give to Caesar what is Caesar's' (Mark 12:17), and he told Pontius Pilate that he, Pilate, had authority only because God had given it to him.

But what if, we may object, the government which has ordered war

Service men and women are trained in obedience

is corrupt, totalitarian and unde-mocratic? What if the war it has entered into does not appear to conform to the principles of a 'just war'? In the maze of decision-making that our rulers struggle through, the righteousness of their decisions is actually their problem. It rests on the conscience of the government. They will make mistakes. They will have mixed mot-ives. They are human, like us. But they are the rulers whom God has sanctioned and at the end of the day they are the rulers whom we have to obey.

How we obey, the manner in which any-one in the services car-ries out their duties, is where the Christian life and witness come into play. This is why it is vitally important that there should be Christians in the Armed Forces, particularly in countries where the military provide a central tool of government. Rejoice that military Christians are emerging and being encouraged in Eastern Europe, in Russia, throughout Africa and Asia, and pray that their godliness will have a profound effect on their fel-lows in the profession of arms.

Alexine Crawford is a Surrey-based freelance writer whose book for BRF on Bible readings for carers is due out later this year.

11

An extract from Faith Odyssey

To boldly go where no Lent book has gone before… BRF's Lent book for 2001, *Faith Odyssey*, takes us on a journey from the ashes of sorrow to shouts of gladness, from slavery to freedom, from being lost to coming home. Each day, passages from the Bible are placed alongside stories drawn from a wide range of literature, TV and film. It is written by the Revd Dr Richard A. Burridge, New Testament scholar, Dean of King's College, London, Series Editor for BRF's *People's Bible Commentary* series. From an early age he has been interested in science fiction.

Ash Wednesday
Stardust and ashes

Have mercy on me, O God, according to your steadfast love; according to your abundant mercy blot out my transgressions. Wash me thoroughly from my iniquity, and cleanse me from my sin. For I know my transgressions, and my sin is ever before me.

Hide your face from my sins, and blot out all my iniquities. Create in me a clean heart, O God, and put a new and right spirit within me. Do not cast me away from your presence, and do not take your holy spirit from me. (Psalm 51:1–3, 10–11)

Therefore I despise myself, and repent in dust and ashes. (Job 42:6)

It was a clear starry night. I lay on my back in the grass on the top of a hill and looked up into the infinite universe above. We were out on an all-night hike with the Scouts, and someone had brought a transistor radio. The peace of the 'wee hours' was broken. 'Ground Control to

Major Tom; Ground Control to Major Tom'—David Bowie's song, 'Space Oddity', drifted out towards those stars. Even if Major Tom had 'something wrong' with his space ship, we knew then that soon our turn would come to travel out into space on our own 'space odyssey'. Even as we watched the sky that night in the late 1960s, somewhere above us Apollo astronauts were on their way to the moon. Within a few decades, we thought we would be all able to do it, as 'scientific man' came of age and set off on the journey to the stars. We were amazed by the scientific discovery that our bodies actually contained within us molecules of heavy elements which had been formed within the gravity of stars. In America, hippies were celebrating at the Woodstock pop festival. Its theme song contained the chorus, 'We are stardust, we are golden, and we've got to get ourselves back to the garden'.

Yet within a few years, it was a different story. The 'love-children' at Woodstock found that they could not get themselves 'back to the garden'. The hippie dream ended bogged down in the mud of Woodstock. Love turned to violence as people were murdered while the Rolling Stones played at a subsequent concert in Altamont. Stardust had turned to ashes, the heavy molecules of long dead stars. David Bowie changed his tune and sang 'Ashes to ashes', in which Major Tom is a junkie, 'strung out in heaven's high, hitting an all-time low'.

The Apollo lunar modules and rover buggies still sit on the moon, undisturbed. We are stuck on this planet, going nowhere.

The biblical writers knew all this. 'In the beginning, when God created the heavens and the earth', he 'formed the man from the dust of the ground' (Genesis 1:1; 2:7). We really are created from dust and ashes, from these molecules which were formed in stars' gravities. The molecules were spread through space when the stars exploded, to end up as part of everything around us. So God warns Adam, 'You are dust and to dust you shall return' (Genesis 3:19). So when we die, we return our molecules to the universe, dust to dust, ashes to ashes. This is the paradox of human existence: we live because God has given us 'the breath of life', but this life is lived in frail bodies, earthen vessels of a few chemicals and water. We should never forget our origins. Even Abraham, the 'friend of God', when he was so bold as to plead with God not to destroy Sodom, knew his human weakness: 'Let me take it upon myself to speak to the Lord, I who am but dust and ashes' (Genesis 18:27).

No wonder that ash became a symbol of repentance, for both individuals and communities. When Job suffered his misfortunes, he 'took a potsherd with which to scrape himself, and sat among the ashes'. He blamed God, for 'he has cast me into the mire, and I have become like dust and ashes'. But when Job has finished his argument with God and heard the Lord's answer out of the whirlwind, he says, 'Therefore I despise myself, and repent in dust and ashes' (Job 2:8; 30:19; 42:6).

Fasting and being clothed in sackcloth and ashes was a way for whole communities to show their repentance. After the preaching of Jonah, 'When the news reached the king of Nineveh, he rose from his throne, removed his robe, covered himself with sackcloth, and sat in ashes' (Jonah 3:6). Jesus upbraided the towns which did not believe in him: 'Woe to you, Chorazin! Woe to you, Bethsaida! For if the deeds of power done in you had been done in Tyre and Sidon, they would have repented long ago in sackcloth and ashes' (Matthew 11:21). Peter recalls the story of Abraham and God's judgment, 'turning the cities of Sodom and Gomorrah to ashes', and warns his readers to repent (2 Peter 2:6). And for all our scientific progress, we now have the capacity to turn all our world's cities to dust and ash.

So here we are at the beginning of the season of Lent. We recall that, despite all our great achievements, we are stardust, the ashes of dead stars, formed from the dust of the ground and the molecules of the universe. We have ash put upon our forehead as a reminder of our frailty and a sign of repentance for our sin. Yet it is also a sign of hope, for God is also the one who 'raises the poor from the dust, and lifts the needy from the ash heap' (Psalm 113:7; 1 Samuel 2:8). The God who created us knows that 'we are but dust' and sent his Son to live among us and to raise us up, back to himself. For the ash used in Ash Wednesday services is traditionally made by burning the old palm crosses from last year. Our Lenten Odyssey is a journey towards Holy Week and Easter, when we shall have new palm crosses as we commemorate Jesus' death for our sin and receive new life through his resurrection. Then our ashes shall be transformed to stardust, not just 'back to the garden' but also beyond the stars 'in heaven's high'.

We are stardust, the ashes of dead stars

For prayer and meditation

*Remember you are dust,
and to dust you shall return.
Turn away from sin
and be faithful to Christ.*

Words used in the Ash Wednesday liturgy when ash is put on to people's foreheads.

An extract from *Taking Hold of Life*

How do we go about making decisions? How can the Bible help us in choosing between right and wrong? *Taking Hold of Life* (available from 16 February) explores the influences that shape our thinking and the difficulty of making moral decisions in the real world. In his foreword for the book, Rob Warner describes it as 'full of practical wisdom for making the most of life.' Author Margaret Killingray is a tutor for the London Institute for Contemporary Christianity, where she contributes to programmes on interpreting the Bible in the modern world.

Living in a good creation
(chapter 17, abridged)

How does the Bible teach us to view our world? … There are a number of possible outlines that would describe a Christian world view, but I want to suggest one that a number of Christian writers have drawn up. This one focuses on the four most important points in the history of God and the world—creation, the fall (that is, the point when evil entered the world), redemption (that is, Jesus' death and resurrection), and the end, the final count-down, the time when God will bring everything to its final conclusion. These form the basis of the Bible story, pull together a great deal of the biblical material and help us to see how it determines our thinking about right and wrong.

The first crucial belief describes how the world as we know it came about—that is, creation. To say that God made the world is only the beginning. Many people would claim this as their belief, but what it actually involves does need spelling out. God existed before there was anything else, and he created the universe and everything that is out of nothing.

At the back of many people's minds as they read this is a misunderstanding about who God is. They have a mental picture of a supreme eternal God, unknowable—perhaps thinking of him as the same God as is worshipped by lots of people all over the world in different ways. They would add on God as Father, Jesus Christ and the Holy Spirit later. But this is not what the Bible says. We cannot simply decide for ourselves what God is like. The Bible has told us who he is. The God who created the world is the trinitarian Christian God—Father, Son and Holy Spirit—and there is no other. All things were made through him, the Bible says about Jesus. Many people use the word 'God' very loosely, but when Christians use the word they should be talking about—as Paul often put it—the God and Father of our Lord Jesus Christ. It is he who made the universe, space, time and all that is.

There is another misunderstanding, and that is that God made the universe and then just set it in motion—winding it up, as it were—and that all the laws of nature, physics and chemistry, evolution and all the developments of social and economic human life simply progressed and produced the world as we know it, with God as an disinterested onlooker. The Bible teaches the very opposite. God is the ongoing, sustaining power behind everything that happens. He is involved in the universe at every level and without his undergirding love it would all collapse into a black hole. These two truths—that God is separate from creation, existed before it and created it all, and that he sustains it and is the force and power within it—are both very important. There are those who believe one of these truths and not the other.

The Bible then goes further and tells us that the universe that God made was good. God took delight in what he had made and enjoyed it. God's final act of creation at the beginning of the world was the making of a human being. God made humans male and female, and he made them in his 'image' and he thought they were very good, too. This means that we are like God in ways that make us different from all the rest of creation. This likeness has been described in many different ways and there have been arguments about exactly what parts of human nature are included in the image of God. But for our purposes

We cannot simply decide for ourselves what God is like

here it is important simply to recognize that in a significant way humans have been set apart by God to relate to him in a way distinct from any other creature.

In addition, humans have been given by God a unique role in the world they inhabit. They are his stewards—responsible, as it were, for the day-to-day running of their whole environment. It is not theirs to do as they like with; they are not bosses or lords with the power to destroy, but carers, gardeners and nurturers.

This doctrine of creation—God as creator and sustainer of a good creation; humans made in the image of God to be stewards of creation—has important consequences for ethics. As we have already implied in the last paragraph, our purpose in being placed in this world is to care for it. This means that much of the recent concern about the environment is an important change of view over the past decades and one that Christians should be part of. They should, of course, have been the leaders of this movement and led the great change in popular thinking. The growing number of people who belong to organizations that care for the natural world and form pressure groups to fight environmentally damaging new proposals are acting ethically within a Christian view of creation care…

But this created world is more than simply the world of nature, the material world around us. Creation also includes human beings, not just as farmers and carers of the environment, but also as social creatures. God has made us social people, and we create cultures, societies and groups of an enormous diversity. We develop law and government, family structures and kinship patterns; we build cities and communications networks; we sing and we dance. These are part of God's creation too, and if individuals are made in God's image, so too are our joint enterprises. But the creation command to be stewards extends to these as well. As Christians, we should not withdraw but work for God in the world, to bring about the Kingdom of God, to seek justice and truth, to fight the abuse of power, to restore human dignity, to bring reconciliation and reconstruction where we can. We should not turn our backs on the communities round us. There too we need to be involved, in the same critical and discerning way as we should be caring for the environment, joining with people of good will who may not be Christian, to change every part of our world into the image of God…

We should not withdraw, but work for God in the world

Donald Coggan— Friend of BRF

The death of Donald Coggan— Lord Coggan of Sissinghurst, former Archbishop of Canterbury— deprived the worldwide Church of one of its most distinguished biblical scholars, and the Bible Reading Fellowship of its President and a lifelong supporter.

Lord Coggan, who died last May at the age of ninety, after a period of increasing physical frailty, had continued that support right up to his final months, completing his last book, *Psalms 73—150* in the People's Bible Commentary series for BRF, shortly before suffering the stroke which ultimately brought about his death. He had been anxious to see the book, a companion to his earlier volume in the same series on Psalms 1—72, completed, regarding it as his 'swansong'—and nothing would have pleased him more than for that 'song' to be a devotional reflection on his beloved Psalms.

Donald Coggan was a Hebrew and Greek scholar

Donald Coggan was a Hebrew and Greek scholar who had devoted the greater part of his distinguished ministry to the study, teaching, translation and preaching of the Bible. He believed passionately in the value of preaching as a means of grace, writing several books on the ministry of preaching, which he saw as essentially 'sacramental'—an 'outward sign' of an inward grace. During his time as Bishop of Bradford and then as Archbishop of York and finally of Canterbury, he encouraged ordinands, parish ministers and Readers to take preaching seriously, and to preach not their own opinions, but the message of the Bible. He believed that there was no greater or more sacred calling than to teach and preach the Bible.

It was with that goal in mind that he became involved—as chairman of the translators' panel—with the translation of the New English Bible, and then, more recently, and in the same role, with its revision in the Revised English Bible. He served as President of the United Bible Societies and founded the College of Preachers. From as long ago as 1946 he had served as a Trustee of BRF and latterly as its President. He took part in the 75th anniversary service in Westminster Abbey and gave a memorable Bible reading at our first BRF 'Authors' Day' in 1998. He and his wife Jean were regular readers of *New Daylight* during their happy years of retirement in Winchester, and she had contributed to its pages from time to time.

Last year, Lord Coggan endorsed BRF's Special Appeal with a ringing call to share the Bible's

No greater or more sacred calling than to teach and preach the Bible

message with a new generation. 'If it is true,' he wrote, 'that "in this, the final age, God has spoken to us in his Son", we should reckon no effort too great to share that truth with a generation whose thought-forms are far removed from those of the first preachers of the Christian faith. That is the work to which BRF is committed, and that is a work every Christian should wholeheartedly support.'

Commenting on Psalm 16 verses 9–11, Donald Coggan wrote, 'These verses take on a richer and fuller meaning when they are seen through the eyes of a Christian rejoicing in the resurrection of Jesus Christ. The believer's "heart is glad", his "hope is sure", his anticipation of life in the presence of God himself is keen. We can be grateful to this happy psalmist for admitting us to the secrets of his confidence and joy.'

'A Christian rejoicing in the resurrection of Jesus Christ'—that is how we shall remember Lord Coggan himself.

The People's Bible Commentary

The stories that appear in 1 and 2 Kings are part of a longer tragedy. Together with the books of Joshua, Judges and Samuel, they tell how the people of Israel moved from a bright beginning across the Jordan River into, and then out of, the promised land, and away to exile in Babylon. This new PBC volume is written by the Revd Dr Stephen B. Dawes who chairs the Cornwall District of the Methodist Church. He formerly taught Old Testament and Hebrew at Trinity College in Ghana and at Queen's College, Birmingham, and continues to do so for the Department of Lifelong Learning of the University of Exeter, as well as writing for *Guidelines*.

1 KINGS 21:17–29

ELIJAH'S CURSE

Elijah, who has had no contact with Ahab and Jezebel since 1 Kings 19:3, receives another command from God to go on a mission and to deliver a message (vv. 17–19). He is to meet Ahab in Naboth's vineyard and confront him with the atrocity that he has committed. He is given two things to say—first, that Ahab has 'murdered' in order to 'possess'. The first verb is the one used in the Sixth Commandment (Exodus 20:13). The second verb is the one used frequently in Deuteronomy

about Israel 'possessing' the land of Canaan. Ahab has 'possessed' a fellow Israelite's 'possession'. The second thing he is given to say is that Ahab will die on the spot on which Naboth died.

The confrontation takes place. After the briefest opening shot from Ahab, Elijah launches into his condemnation. Ahab knows from whom he has come and on whose behalf he speaks, so there is no need for Elijah to preface his words with 'Thus says the Lord'. The Lord will bring the same total disaster upon his house that has already come on that of Jeroboam (1 Kings 15:29–30) and Baasha (1 Kings 16:11). In this case, however, the Lord has a special word for the queen. She has been the cause of much of the evil that has been done, and she will die because of it.

Verses 25–26 read like part of the standard obituaries which the northern kings receive, noting that Ahab was, in fact, the worst of them all. Others had permitted or encouraged the use of idols in the worship of the Lord, or the worship of other gods. Ahab has been so bad that he is compared with the Amorites, one of the main ethnic groups occupying Canaan before the Israelites. The NRSV puts these verses in brackets and calls them an evaluation by the writer which breaks the connection between verses 24 and 27. That is not necessary. These verses serve to point out that Elijah's curse on Ahab and Jezebel is completely justified and to prepare for the unexpected turn of events in verses 27–29.

'Repentance' and 'forgiveness'

Most religions recognize a distinction between right and wrong, and have ways of dealing with wrongdoing. These will include a variety of preventative measures and means to neutralize the power of evil. There will be ways to give a new start to those who see the error of their ways and a system of sanctions against those who do not.

Ahab, either because he recog-

nizes the truth about himself or because he is terrified by the sanctions about to come into force, 'humbles himself' before God. He expresses his penitence in fasting and in wearing a sackcloth under-shirt. Fasting and the use of sackcloth are two ways of expressing penitence for wrongdoing, but the final phrase in verse 28 indicates that something inward is required as well. The translations vary but the point is that Ahab feels remorse or regret. He is sorry, though the phraseology in verse 29 rather suggests that Elijah needs to be convinced that this sorrow is genuine.

We are told that because of this repentance the threatened disaster will now take place in his son's reign instead of in his. The punishment on Jeroboam and Baasha had not, in fact, taken effect in their lifetime but in that of their sons.

Some might wonder, however, why the disaster should now take place at all. Has not Ahab been forgiven? Does not forgiveness mean a new start with the slate wiped clean? The Deuteronomic response to that question would be to say that it is not as simple as that. We might answer the question by pointing out that acts have consequences, and that for some forms of wrongdoing at least, although forgiveness can and does take away the guilt involved, it cannot take away the consequences. That is a hard lesson which the Deuteronomic Historians, in their own way, insist that we must learn.

Profile—Margaret Sentamu

Recent statistics of Church of England attendance have caused much handwringing and doom and gloom. Many people feel that, as much as anybody, it's the job of the clergy to make a difference—but how do you go about choosing somebody to take on such a daunting task? To a large extent, it is Margaret Sentamu and her colleagues in the C of E's Ministry Division who have that very job.

Margaret is Senior Selection Secretary, heading up the work of what used to be known as ABM (and, before that, ACCM). Hers is the department of the Ministry Division which is responsible for choosing who will, and who will not, go forward for ordination training. Her work is based at Church House, the national headquarters of the C of E, in the shadow of Westminster Abbey.

The Ministry Division oversees everything to do with church ministry—vocations, Reader training, ministry among the deaf, education, training, finance, and deployment. It was set up as a result of the Turnbull Commission (headed up

Leadership skills are not just desirable but essential

by Michael Turnbull, Bishop of Durham and Vice-President of BRF), when a proper C of E management structure was established for the first time, overseen by the new Archbishops' Council.

So what sort of people is Margaret's department seeking for ministry in the 21st century? A leaflet is available, summarizing the criteria: candidates have to be familiar with Anglican practices, able to explain their sense of calling to ministry, having a personal commitment to Christ and to their local church. They should also be mature and self-aware, and leadership skills are not just desirable but essential. And

22

they must be prepared to cope with the emotional and intellectual demands of the training.

More applications are needed from ethnic minority groups and from men and women under 30, to help counterbalance the recent tendency for ordinands to be slightly older. Margaret stresses that older candidates are still welcome, although inevitably they have fewer years to offer the church after their training is finished:

We do want those who can offer a long stint of service and grow as the future leadership of the church.

We are looking for people who have vision and energy, and are flexible in their approach. And they need to be people who believe that they have good news to share, who are excited about their faith.

Margaret thinks that the main challenge facing priests today is our rapidly changing culture, with its atmosphere of uncertainty caused by rapid technological advance:

Society is so fluid, so individualistic now. People's jobs are no longer secure, and then there is the post-modern scene. Priests need to be able to cope with all that and continue to have something to say.

She adds, however, that *all* Christians have a vocation, not just those who end up being ordained:

Our calling comes through baptism, when we are initiated into the church. Some are called to be ordained priests, some to be deacons, and some called to lay discipleship. Others are called to work in the family, the community, in industry. God doesn't just call people to church-based jobs!

While church ministry has traditionally focused on the ordained person—the so-called 'Father knows best' syndrome—the focus is turning towards working in partnership with clergy:

There has been a huge shift in models of priestly ministry and how people perceive it. There is the highly pastoral model—visiting, carrying out the 'occasional offices' [baptisms, weddings, funerals]—and there is the model of the leader who enables and facilitates the work of lay people. Both models are still valid, though, and neither should look down on the other.

Margaret herself has more than 25 years of first-hand experience of church ministry. Born and raised in Uganda, she studied literature and education at university there and taught for a while before coming to the UK in the early 1970s, when her then barrister husband went to study theology in Cambridge. She took time out to raise her family (a son and a daughter) but was also involved in voluntary work in her husband's parishes as well as helping to select people to work with mission agencies, such as CMS and USPG.

Her interest in education has continued, and she recently completed an MA in Adult Education. Her long-term goal is to help facilitate adult learning in church-based contexts:

Adults learn through doing, not just through being preached at. They tell stories, reflect on their experiences, drawing lessons that turn into action.

Since 1996 her husband, John, has been Bishop of Stepney. Margaret's attitude is:

I am married to a bishop but I am not a bishop's wife in the traditional sense!

An old-fashioned world of floral frocks and garden parties is not to her taste:

You have to be yourself and exercise your gifts and ministry in combination with the person to whom you are married. If you give up too much, you are hurting yourself and you may end up resenting your husband or wife.

She is fully aware of the particular pressures of being 'married to the church':

There is a high degree of sacrifice involved. Being a public person —both you and the members of your family—takes up emotional energy.

There is a financial sacrifice too, especially when people give up highly paid jobs to enter ordained ministry. And there is a significant element of stress:

A lot of clergy are under a lot of stress. The job is relentless and the individual has to work out how to make time for themselves and for their family.

On the other hand, the job has many positive aspects:

You have a very unique and special position as somebody in public, representative ministry. You represent God to the people and the people to God. You disciple people, see them grow. Yes, there are enormous frustrations but they can be outweighed by joy.

Naomi Starkey

The letter to the Romans

Paul's epistle to the Romans has the reputation of a mountain. Layers of argument are stacked one upon another, stretching our minds out of their normal range of thought and concern, promising to leave us mentally breathless should we start to ascend. Yet, like many a mountain, this letter takes a grip on the climber. Our spirits are lifted, we discover a wider and grander perspective on the work of God, and we return to these slopes time and again, to taste the clean, sharp air of the gospel.

Like so much of the best Christian thinking, Romans arises from a concern for mission. Paul is a mature missionary, at a point of transition in his own career (15:23). Behind him are sharp controversies, when he fought to win recognition from Jewish Christians for his new Gentile churches (Acts 15; Galatians 2). As he writes, he has just taken a collection among these new fellowships, to relieve poverty in the Jerusalem church; this gift of money will be a visible sign of Christian respect and friendship. Ahead of him is a new phase of gospel work: he wants to go west, to Spain, and to use the church in Rome as a stepping stone, to support that venture (15:24). Yet as he looks to Rome, reports about the situation there echo his own great concern for unity—for this seems itself to be a divided church.

So Paul's letter has two great passions: to explain how Christians belong to Christ, and how they belong to each other. It is a profoundly evangelical document, concerned with the gospel, God's good news (1:16). It is also a thoroughly ecumenical letter, a truly catholic epistle, binding Christians together in love and mutual understanding. These two great concerns are plaited together throughout. Because of the gospel—what God has done in Jesus Christ—the church has the right and duty to overcome its divisions, and show the world a new kind of human community.

Romans is theology—serious thought about the ways of God. It is missionary—laying out the good news Paul is urgent to spread. It is pastoral—for Paul's teaching will help this fragmented and multi-racial congregation to renew its confidence and claim its unity, in Jesus Christ.

We begin at the end, and meet the Roman church. Then we go back to the beginning, and follow Paul's letter through.

1   Saints divided   *Read Romans 16*

No other New Testament letter ends with quite so many personal greetings. Here is a cloud of memories from Paul's missionary travels: loyal co-workers (v. 4); an early convert (v. 5); some who suffered with him (v. 7); one who helped him (v. 13). Even the list of names tells us a good deal about this church.

Paul mentions some Jewish friends (vv. 7, 13), but most of the names he lists were common among Gentiles, typically among slaves or freed slaves. This is a racially mixed church, and mainly a church of the poorer or middle classes. Here are active Christians, energetic and practical. Paul refers often to their 'work' for Christ (vv. 3, 6, 9, 12). Several of the workers Paul mentions are women. This is not a fellowship where all the responsibility is taken by men.

Sadly Romans 16 appears to show a divided church. Paul greets 'the church in their house' (v. 5); we hear of 'the brothers and sisters who are with them' (v. 14), and 'the saints who are with them' (v. 15). This company of Christians creates the impression of a scattered fleet of ships, each one with its own captain, company and course.

There are clues to this situation in literature of the period. The first Christians in Rome were Jewish. By AD49 the growth of this Christian fellowship led to trouble among the city's Jewish community, and the government responded with an expulsion order (Acts 18:2). When Jews started trickling back to Rome, the Christians among them found that the church had mushroomed. But it was full of Gentiles, with a pattern of worship and witness that took little account of Jewish sensitivities. Jewish Christians felt unwelcome, so they started meeting separately. They felt—as Jewish Christians sometimes feel today—like a community in-between. Their Christian beliefs had separated them from their Jewish friends, and now their Jewishness made them feel like strangers in the predominantly Gentile Christian church.

This epistle to the Romans aims to repair—or at least to bridge—that division in the church. It does so by a fresh and powerful exposition of the gospel of God's love.

2   Man with a mission   *Read Romans 1:1–15*

The letter opens with a personal introduction. Rome was the hub of communication in the ancient world—all roads led to it. For Paul it will be a staging post on the journey to Spain, but also a preaching station (v. 11). Some Christians there have never met him. So to win their confidence and support, he starts by presenting himself and summarizing his message.

- *Man on a mission (v. 1). Paul is a man with a purpose, sent by God to spread the gospel. The Master he serves, and the message he carries, matter more than any details of his personal life.*

- *Past and present (v. 2). The gospel is not a divine 'plan', thought up by God after the failure of earlier schemes. But Old and New Testaments form one coherent story of love. The good news of Jesus is the fulfilment of ancient promise.*

- *Genes and glory (vv. 3, 4). The career of Jesus—God's incarnate and risen Son—had two phases. He came as Israel's Messiah, born into a Jewish heritage. Yet the resurrection gave his work a wider reach and a fuller power.*

- *Obedience and faith (v. 5). Paul's wording is 'the obedience of faith'. God sent Jesus, and raised Jesus from death; now he wants people to believe in Jesus. So faith is our response to God's purpose. It is the heart of all Christian obedience, the first mark of the church's life.*

- *Israel and the Gentiles (v. 5). God's love is for all nations. The good news ripples outwards like waves on a pond. The Messiah promised to the Jews becomes the Lord proclaimed to the world. That does not erase God's ancient promise; it extends it.*

- *You and Christ (v. 6). The reach of this gospel has gathered the Roman Christians into a wide and holy fellowship. They are part of one great company in Christ. They are 'saints' (v. 7), intimately joined to the life and purpose of God.*

So Paul rejoices in the faith of these Christians (v. 8), prays for them (v. 9), and longs to visit them (v. 10). He wants to enjoy their friendship (v. 12), and to spread the faith among them (v. 13). A sense of duty and of debt beckons him forward (v. 14). His eagerness in his work is bound up with his concern for the church (v. 15)—and both flow from his love for Christ.

3   World awry   *Read Romans 1:16–32*

Now we leave the prologue of the letter and start to travel into the main argument. Verses 16 and 17 stand as a headline over the whole epistle, a signpost towards the destination in view, a summary of the Christian gospel: This is a message of 'salvation', of human wholeness and security in the love of God. It is a gospel of equality, that addresses Jew and Gentile and binds them together in the service of God. And it reaches 'from faith to faith': it comes out of the solid faithfulness of God, and invites the faith of men and women, from every nation and race. For all these reasons Paul is 'not ashamed', not embarrassed or alarmed by criticism, but happy to tell of God's open and glad tidings.

But before we come round to joy, we must set off in the opposite direction. For verses 18–32 show the background to the gospel, the diagnosis for which Christ is the cure, the maze of human experience, out of which there is no through road to God except via the cross. This gloomy passage matches some Jewish criticisms of the Gentile world—which attacked, for example, the worship of animal statues (v. 23). It also echoes the concerns of Gentile philosophers for what was 'rational' (v. 20), 'natural' (v. 26) and 'proper' (v. 28). But these verses are much more than local prejudice: when Paul writes of people refusing to know God (v. 19), exchanging the truth of God for a lie (v. 25), and reaping the harvest that is death (v. 32), he strikes a deep resonance with the story of Adam and Eve in Genesis 3. This is the common stuff of human nature.

Verses 26 and 27 have sometimes been picked out and used in debates about Christian attitudes to homosexual practice. Paul clearly thought of homosexual activity as one symptom of a world gone awry, but he never describes this as the only sin in the world.

The root of all evil, as Romans 1 tells it, is a basic human reluctance to give God the honour he deserves (v. 21). That involves us all, and affects us all.

4 Religious sins *Read Romans 2*

All the world—or at least much of the press, and some of our neighbours—loves a scandal in the church. Christians, who preach goodness and try to practise it, are easy targets when we stumble. That vulnerability can make it hard for us to be honest with ourselves, to admit that we are often not very holy. We are entangled in the sinfulness of the human race, and need forgiveness as surely as anyone else does.

That is the point of Romans 2. There is no safe vantage point from which we can look at the contradictions and compromises of human life, and think that we are not involved (v. 1). Religion should not blind us to our own failures, our own part in the tangles of chapter 1. God watches how we walk, not just how we talk. Hard hearts, that criticize others without repenting of their own sins, are storing up trouble for themselves (vv. 3–5). God's fair and impartial judgment (vv. 9–11) reflects what we do with the light we have (vv. 12–16).

The second half of the chapter has Jewish readers especially in mind. They had a long tradition of living under God's grace. The custom of circumcision marked all their sons with the sign of covenant love. Their law was meant to keep them true and holy. Yes, Paul will say later, these things are good, and they came from God. But in chapter 2 he stresses the difference between privilege and presumption, between what you have been given in the past and what you take for granted in the future.

A religious background does not mean much unless there is a true life to match it (vv. 17–24). Tradition and heritage are always hollow, unless they are filled out by a lively inner godliness (vv. 25–29). Some of Paul's language is deliberately strong, for effect: what he said would not apply to all Jews in equal measure. But his point is that Jewish people, even with their ancient law, would still need the gospel. And so do we.

So Romans 2 need not demean and dispirit us. Properly understood, it can give us fresh courage to be honest with ourselves. However far advanced we are in Christian faith, we still need to be pardoned. And however badly we stumble, we shall not be out of range of God's forgiveness.

5 Set right with God *Read Romans 3*

The chapter begins with a string of questions (vv. 1–8), which the previous paragraphs have raised. First (vv. 1–4), if Jews and Gentiles are both subject to the temptation and taint of sin, what advantage has the Jew? What has become of their ancient privilege? What good did it do? Then second (vv. 5–8), is it not odd—and even unfair—that God can use human sin as a way of showing his character and truth? What incentive is left for our doing good?

Paul will tackle these questions squarely and frankly: the first little clutch in chapters 9—11, the second in chapter 6. But for the moment he brushes them aside, with only hints of what his answers will be. He does not want readers to be distracted from the main thrust of the argument. The whole of humanity is involved in sin, 'under sin' (v. 9), snared by its guilt and by its intrusive interference in our lives. Jew and Gentile stand side by side in God's plan of salvation (1:17). But as background to that salvation, they are equal before judgment (2:9, 10), and together under sin (3:9). A string of quotations from the Jewish scriptures emphasizes the point (3:10–18).

In verse 21 we start to move from darkness to light, from tragedy to rescue. God has stepped in, in Jesus Christ (v. 22). Here we feel the pulse of Romans, and come near to the heart of God:

- *'Witnessed by the law' (v. 21). Christ's coming is the completion and hope of the Old Testament, not an abrupt novelty but a fulfilment of what has gone before.*

- *'Without distinction' (v. 22). The Christian message meets Gentile and Jew on equal terms. It is not limited by ancient boundaries.*

- *'For all who believe (v. 22)… as a gift' (v. 24). The gospel works through people trusting what God has done for them. There is no earning, deserving or purchasing involved. The price has been paid, by Jesus Christ.*

- *'By Christ's blood' (v. 25). The cross was the place where God's mercy met human sin. Jesus was not some helpless middle-man, but a true mediator, bearing the pain of our reconciliation. Against the murky background of human sin, God has set the stark clarity of the cross, so that darkness may be swallowed up by light and sin pardoned by love.*

6   Father of faith   *Read Romans 4*

The death of Jesus is God's new way of putting people right with himself (3:24). This gospel works through faith, not through the ancient Jewish law (3:28). Yet Paul is keen to explain that the message of faith has deep roots in Israel's scripture, and that a multi-racial Christian Church is a proper fulfilment of God's long-term plan.

Enter Abraham, hero of the Old Testament. He was known as the model man of faith, who trusted God's promise even when all life's probabilities seemed stacked against him. He was also the prototype Jew, the great forefather of the nation of Israel. So Paul uses Abraham as an example, to show what faith can mean. Yet the Abraham story also helps Paul to anchor the Christian message in the Old Testament, and to show the Roman Christians that their faith comes out of an ancient Jewish heritage.

This chapter proceeds in four movements:

- *Abraham's faith was what set him right with God (vv. 3–8, drawing on Genesis 15:6). His relationship with God was based on trust, love and pardon, not on demand, deserving or debt.*

- *Abraham trusted God long before he was circumcised (vv. 9–12, referring again to Genesis 15:6, and to Genesis 17). So he is a father figure for all who believe, Jews and Gentiles alike.*

- *Abraham was always meant as an international figure, a 'father of many nations' (vv. 13–17a). A Church that goes back to Abraham is a Church for the whole world (Genesis 12:3).*

- *Abraham had trusted that God would give him and Sarah a child, even though they were past the normal age for a family (vv. 17b–22). Christian faith too is based on the coming of life when all seemed dead, in the resurrection of Jesus (vv. 23–25).*

So the Christian gospel is like Abraham's relationship with God: based on trust; not dependent on race; international in perspective and potential; and centred on the resurrection power of God. It comes from the distant past, yet is bright with the promise of new life.

GUIDELINES

The tight argument of Romans can be intimidating. If we find ourselves overwhelmed by detail, it is good to remember the main purpose. For Romans is about 'the gospel of God' (1:1). William Tyndale, who translated the Bible into English in the sixteenth century, wrote, 'Gospel is a Greek word, and signifieth good, merry, glad and joyful tidings, that maketh a man's heart glad, and maketh him sing, dance and leap for joy.' We too may rejoice, in this message of free forgiveness, costly love, steady trust, and resurrection hope.

God of wisdom,
    you stretch our minds with your truth.
God of love,
    you beckon our faith from your cross.
God of surprises,
    you stir us to rejoicing by your Spirit.
God of good news,
    we offer you our praise.
Through Jesus Christ our Lord. Amen

1   **Starting again**   *Read Romans 5*

The first half of Romans 5, up to verse 11, has been compared to
a railway junction. So many lines of thought run through it. It is a
meeting point for several important ideas, and a transition stage in
the long connected argument of Romans.

'Justification' (v. 1) means being claimed by God as his people,
welcomed into a sure and secure relationship. This relationship is
more than just a legal belonging, but is nourished by grace, by
present experience of God's goodness, and by a steady hope that
we shall one day know God's glory more clearly and fully than
now (v. 2). So in the trials and pains that life brings—both those
that arrive as our common human lot, and those that come out of
our Christian commitment—the Christian may rejoice and be
glad. For God will use even suffering to shape and strengthen our
faith, to draw us to himself, and to acquaint us with his love (vv.
3–5).

Hope comes from the cross of Christ. This visible sign assures
us that God's love has been given deliberately and permanently
(vv. 6–8). The Christian is lastingly reconciled to God by Christ's
death (vv. 9–11), drawn into God's friendship and care, and able
to look forward without fear.

More than that, Christ has brought a new pattern to our human
living. The second half of this chapter, from verse 12 onwards,
contrasts Jesus and Adam. There are two asides—in verses 13–14
and in verse 20; these concern the Jewish law, and they make
Paul's line of argument rather harder to trace. Once they are
filtered out, the main thread becomes clearer.

But even the main thread may read oddly to modern minds,
who have been taught to think of Adam and Eve as just an ancient
fable. If that oddness strikes you, it may help you to notice that
Adam is the background to these verses, but the foreground is
Christ. Recall too that even a good fable is a window into reality:
Adam stands for Everyone, for your life and mine.

Paul describes Adam as the prototype human, a template for
the rest of us. His first act of disobedience (vv. 12 and 18, referring

to Genesis 3) set a pattern for everyone else. His trespass mired and obscured the path, so that we lose our way. We share his fallen humanity, and our life too becomes perishable and mortal, cursed with death as his was (Genesis 2:17).

Now Jesus reverses that curse, offering the free gift of 'justification' (vv. 15–17), a life right with God. His obedience (vv. 18, 19)—especially in his dying (Mark 14:36)—opens the way to eternal life (v. 21), and sets a new pattern of right and holy living for his people to follow. That will be the theme of chapter 6.

2 Service contract *Read Romans 6*

This chapter takes up a question posed earlier in 3:8: Why be good? If God saves sinners, if the depth of human sin actually shows the wealth of God's grace and love, if indeed Christ has died to pardon our wrongdoing, why bother to do right (v. 1)?

The answer follows on from chapter 5. The Christian no longer belongs to the segment of human life that has been patterned by Adam's sin, but to the company of people that is shaped by Christ's obedient death. The cross is a milestone for the Christian, leaving behind the old era of wrongdoing, and opening a new road of right living (v. 7). It would be unnatural for a Christian to follow sinful ways; that would be a step into the past.

Two pictures are used to explain this, in verses 3–11 and 12–23. The first is Christian baptism, which draws the Christian into sharing the death of Christ (v. 3), and beckons us through into the life of the resurrection (v. 4). The deep waters of immersion baptism, as practised in many churches, display this with special clarity. But 'whatever mode of baptism is used'—sprinkling, pouring or immersion—'the symbolic truth of dying to the old life and rising to the new remains' (John Stott). Baptism commissions and launches the Christian into a new lifestyle. It speaks of new loyalty and new possibility.

The second picture (vv. 12–23) is slavery, the committed service of a human life to a master's will. The Roman world of Paul's time knew the image very well: people belonged to others, without choice or freedom. But everyone, says Paul, is a slave—not all to a human master, but none of us is truly free and self-controlled. The powerful desires, temptations, patterns of behaviour and currents of convention that swirl around us mean that none of us is able to steer a truly straight course. We go with the flow, often against our better judgment; Paul calls it 'slavery to sin' (v. 17). The big difference in being a Christian is that our loyalty is pledged to a different direction, to obedience, to righteousness and to holiness (vv. 16–19). Gradually, and curiously, this new slavery starts to feel like freedom (v. 18). Christian commitment loosens the suffocating grip of wrongdoing, and opens the wide vistas of eternal life (vv. 22–23).

3 Split personality *Read Romans 7*

Suddenly the story takes a new turn. Chapter 6 was about two patterns of living, sin and righteousness. Now in chapter 7 the main theme is law. Paul wants his readers to realize that there is a difference between following the Jewish law and living the Christian life. He is convinced that the gospel is a thing of lively and animating power, not just a written code of commands (v. 6).

So the first few verses speak of the Christian as a person who has moved, from one world to another. A new life has begun. The law, which was part of the old era, loses its claim on the Christian, because the Christian belongs to a new world, to the risen Christ (vv. 1–6). Now it is the Holy Spirit who shapes Christian behaviour and lifestyle (v. 6), and who helps us to activate the pattern of righteous life described in chapter 6.

But that raises a sharp question—especially for Jewish readers—about the relationship between gospel and law. 'Does Paul despise the law?' some might ask (v. 7). 'Does he look on it as a wasteful, miserable, sinful thing?' Paul's answer is balanced, yet also passionate.

The law was not a wrong thing, he says, but a holy and spiritual thing (vv. 7, 12, 14). However, it pointed to a depth and quality of righteousness that it could not produce. Human nature is 'flesh': we are frail and sometimes pathetically susceptible to temptation (v. 14). The effect of law is to sharpen our awareness of sin (v. 7), and sometimes that actually inflames the sin it forbids—especially with sins of the mind and heart such as coveting (vv. 8–11).

So a sensitive and godly person can become a divided person (vv. 15–20), longing to follow the commandments of God, but often straying—even when that was not the intention—and hurting inwardly as the struggle continues. The law itself seems double-edged, promising life yet seeming to lack real motive power. It reckons to chart the sea of life; but in order to sail, you need the breath of the wind.

So this chapter speaks of the limitations of life under the Jewish law, and shows how these contrast with the life of the Spirit, in the following chapter. Paul deliberately targets the perspectives of his first readers. Yet countless Christians of more recent times have felt that Romans 7 surfaces in their own living. We do not respond as we ought to God's Spirit; we are often frail, false and fallible when we try to follow the ways of God; our victories are partial but never final. We may be Christ's people at heart, but we have to struggle and wrestle, to learn to live his way.

4 Breath of life *Read Romans 8:1–17*

Chapter 8 is the antidote to chapter 7. The law could not lead people to holy living, for it was constantly hampered by the weaknesses of human nature. But in Christ God has dealt with sin, loosened its grip on human living, and put a new possibility before us—life in the Spirit (vv. 2–3). Romans 6 is the pattern, Romans 8 the path—'live by the Spirit, set your mind on the Spirit' (v. 5). Romans 7 was a false trail, a cul-de-sac. Romans 8 is an open road.

The central character in chapter 8 is the Holy Spirit—'the Spirit of God… the Spirit of Christ' (v. 9), 'the Spirit of him who raised Jesus from the dead… his Spirit that dwells in you' (v. 11). The Spirit is the living presence and power of Jesus, moulding our living closer to the pattern of Jesus Christ (vv. 2, 4, 6). The Spirit is also a bridge, between the daily life of the Christian and the hope ahead. Hope came to meet the world in the death and resurrection of Jesus. But that hope becomes real for us, strikes root in our lives, through the Holy Spirit who dwells within us (v. 11). The Spirit gives us confidence that we belong to God (v. 16), and the Spirit stirs the hope within us that the life we now have in Jesus is a seed, the start, of something greater, fuller and more enduring and glorious than any experience on earth (v. 17).

In the Science Museum in London, in the children's gallery, is a giant saucer—a yard across—set on its side. It sits on a little rostrum, a few feet above the crowd. It's not wired, or electronic, it's just a solid metal dish. At the far end of the room, perhaps twenty yards away, is another dish facing the first one. There is a marker at the centre of each dish. And if you put your face beside the marker of one dish and speak in a gentle and natural voice, while your friend listens beside the marker of the other dish, the voice comes through, calm and clear. Over all the hubbub of excited children, the rushing about, the hum of people and machines, the sound of a human voice gets through.

Of course science has an explanation: the sound waves take form as a broad parallel beam, and are reflected to a point by the second dish. But there is an illustration here too. Something like this is meant, when Romans 8:16 says that 'the Spirit bears witness with our spirit that we are children of God'. Over the clamour and chaos of a busy world, amid the myriad voices that surround us, God's quiet voice—from far away, and yet near to us as our own breath—assures us that we are part of his new world, his new work.

5 Breath of life *Read Romans 8:18–39*

As I write the Christmas cards are coming in, and they bring mixed and varied tidings. Friends write of their year. Grief, trouble and worry figure all too frequently. 'The sufferings of this present time' (v. 18) are a major element of our lives. How then do Christians meet suffering?

We suffer 'with Christ' (v. 17). The Christian never suffers alone, but the Lord who suffered for us on the cross now lives in us (v. 10), sensitive to our distress, loving us through the darkness.

We suffer as part of creation (vv. 19–23). Decay (v. 21) and waste (v. 20) claim and damage too much of God's good handiwork. Creation aches and groans, like a mother giving birth, longing for the renewal of its life, for purpose to come out of its pain (v. 22). The Spirit too is a voice of expectancy, coming to Christians as the first instalment of greater blessing ahead (v. 23), prompting us to long for God's renewing touch. Eventually, in some mysterious way, the resurrection of Christ's people will bring a kind of resurrection for creation too (vv. 19, 21). The world was made to laugh, not to weep, and one day it will be given the laughter of Christ.

We suffer as people whose prayers are heard, even when we cannot put those prayers into words of our own. The Holy Spirit is an interpreter, making our needs known in the heart of God (vv. 26–27), as surely as he makes God's love known to us (v. 16).

We are confident that suffering is not the end (vv. 28–30). God is faithful. When he calls a person to faith, he begins a long-term project in that person's life, which he means to complete, in our mortal life and in the glory that is ahead.

We suffer as people who are loved. Every misfortune, oppression and distress (vv. 35–39) is overshadowed by the love of Christ, by his cross (v. 32), resurrection and concern for his people (v. 34). We suffer in the security of God's love in Christ, and nothing can separate us from that love.

That assurance sends us into God's troubled world, to bear its burdens, to reshape it for good, to love in the name of Jesus, and to live in a way that points forward, to God's coming glory.

6   God and Israel: the past   *Read Romans 9:1–29*

If you belong to a family in which few of your close relatives share your faith, even though background and upbringing have given them every opportunity, then you may have a fellow-feeling for the opening verses of chapter 9. Paul grieves for his own family, for the Jewish nation to which he belonged and whose heritage he honours and reveres. This people lived under God's love, the Messiah was born among them, they were intended to share God's goodness with the world (vv. 4–5), but most of them have not responded to the gospel of their Messiah. Paul longs for them to recognize and believe what God has been doing among them (vv. 2–3). It hurts him bitterly that so many of his fellow Jews seem to have missed the point and purpose of their heritage.

These three chapters, Romans 9—11, explore the mystery of God's dealings with Israel. Today's section traces the story through the Old Testament. First, says Paul, God has always dealt with a narrow line within Israel: 'Not all who are from Israel belong to Israel' (v. 6). God picked out a definite track through the nation's history, giving life when there seemed no future (vv. 7–9), inviting trust in his promises rather than working automatically by genes and family trees. Grace was covenanted, but never to be presumed upon. Esau may have forfeited his own birthright (Genesis 25:29–34; 27:1–40), but behind the choice of Jacob was the strange and inscrutable purpose of God (vv. 10–13). Paul finds nothing novel or inconsistent, if some Jews seem to have discovered God's good news, while others have been passed by.

Yet even in this, God is not unfair or ungracious (v. 14). We cannot tell God how to do his job (vv. 19–21). He has complete right to choose how and where he advances his purpose (vv. 15–18). But we may hold on to the promises of his love. For God's love can come where people have ceased to expect it (vv. 25–26). God's work is never rubbed out or ruined; there is always a remnant that he can revive (vv. 27–29). We may not take God's favour for granted—but with God we need never say that all is lost.

GUIDELINES

I always look on Romans 5—8 as the centre of this epistle. Put right with God by faith, beckoned and baptised into a new pattern of behaviour, led by the Spirit of Christ and held securely within God's love—this the life that God sets before us in Jesus Christ. This life stretches into glory ahead (5:2; 8:18), it looks forward to the renewing of God's world in Christ (8:20–21), and it comes from the cross (5:9–10) and risen life (6:5; 8:34) of the Son of God.

> *Praise be to Jesus Christ,*
> *in whose cross is pardon,*
> *in whose resurrection is power,*
> *in whose Spirit is promise,*
> *and in whose love is the sure grasp of God upon us.*
> *Amen.*

1   God and Israel: the present   *Read Romans 9:30—10:21*

The long account of God's dealings with Israel continues. But this
chapter shifts the focus in two important respects. First, it
concerns the present, Paul's own day, whereas most of chapter 9
was looking back. Second, it looks from below (as it were) at
human response to God, rather than tracing (as if from above) the
contours of God's purpose.

The irony is (9:31—10:4) that Israel, a zealous, religious and
committed people, has largely overlooked her Messiah. Jesus came
as the climax and culmination of Israel's history (v. 4). Yet Gentiles
have flocked to the gospel in much greater numbers than Jews (v.
30). The people of Israel's mistake, says Paul, is that they have
failed to see the law as a stimulus to faith. They have been
concerned for 'works' (v. 32)—which may refer especially to those
outward ceremonies such as circumcision, diet and sabbath,
which separated and distinguished Israel from other nations. So
their law has become a self-contained system, rather than a lens
for looking beyond itself to the gospel.

There is a great difference between a relationship based on
doing and one based on believing (10:5–10). The law operated
through what people did (v. 5); the gospel rests on what Jesus has
done (v. 9). Paul quotes from the Old Testament in order to
explain how accessible the gospel is (10:8, 11–13). The message
is available, and depends only on the work of messengers (v. 15),
to carry it freely to Jew and Gentile alike (v. 12). Yet as messengers
have taken the word (v. 18), the response has been very mixed.
Indeed the Jewish response has been predominantly negative
(v. 21).

Chapter 11 will begin to look ahead, to reflect on God's coming
plans for Israel. But perhaps chapter 10 invites us first to examine
ourselves. We too can sometimes allow our customs and moral
commitments to become a law unto themselves, rather than a
window on to the purposes of God. These paragraphs remind us
to see church custom in the light of Christ, so that we do not live
as an ingrown clique but as an open company of pilgrims. Then

indeed our lives may make God's message widely and freely known. And that may be a small step towards overcoming the grievous gulf that still exists between Jews and Christians.

2 God and Israel: the prospect   *Read Romans 11*

Chapter 10 ended in frustration and grief (10:21), lamenting the unwillingness of Jewish people to receive the good news about their Messiah. Then as counterpoint to this sorrow, chapter 11 clings on to the faithfulness of God: however thin the believing remnant in Israel, God's purpose is one of hope and grace. God will never erase his people's life (vv. 1–6). Though the nation may seem to have stumbled and fallen away (vv. 11–12), Paul holds three positive themes before his readers, as he probes the purposes of God:

- *Envy (vv. 13–14). Paul actually wants to irritate his Jewish kinsfolk, to provoke them into realizing what they have missed, when they see the enthusiastic faith of the Gentile churches.*

- *Expectancy (vv. 15–16). If the Jews' refusal to believe the gospel has resulted in so many Gentiles finding their way to faith, surely something far grander can be expected, if only Israel will turn to Christ.*

- *Dependence (vv. 17–24). Gentile Christians should remember that they are guests, adopted into the Jewish family of faith. The stock of the tree is planted in Old Testament soil. So though Gentile branches have now been introduced, there would still be nothing unnatural—quite the reverse!—in Jewish boughs being grafted back into the stem (v. 24).*

From verse 25 the chapter moves to a grand and glorious climax, recalling God's ancient choice of Israel (vv. 28–29) and his constant mercy (vv. 30–32). The people of Israel have not finished with God, nor he with them. These verses surely encourage Paul's readers to go on telling their Jewish neighbours about the Messiah Jesus (v. 31; cf. v. 14). But for all our human effort and explaining, the mystery and mercy remain with God (vv. 33–36). That mercy will one day bring together a company of Christians, Jew and

Gentile, whose racial make-up will majestically affirm God's patient and early work among the Jews (vv. 26, 32).

So this long discussion of Israel's place in God's purpose ends in praise and awe (v. 36). It has been said that the pattern in history is only visible from the reverse side; we can never really see what God is up to. That view is not quite fair, as an account of these chapters. The God of the Bible is indeed wreathed in mystery (v. 33), and those who serve him may encounter both disappointment (10:1) and blessed and unexpected surprise (9:30). But God is also steadfastly faithful, and as we commit ourselves to sharing his work, that faithfulness should give us a holy optimism about the long-term outcome (11:32, 36).

3 Commitment for life   *Read Romans 12*

The single word 'therefore' (v. 1) marks a shift into the final main section of the letter, into three chapters of practical instruction about Christian living. The first theme is commitment. Because of what God has done, because of all that the preceding chapters have explained, the Christian is to live as a person committed to God. The language is very physical—'your bodies as a living sacrifice' (v. 1)—and this emphasizes how deeply the Christian life claims the activity and service of our strength and days. Yet the word 'sacrifice' also suggests praise and thanks, for Christian life is based on the sacrificial death of Jesus. When we give ourselves to God, we are responding to Christ's giving of himself for us. This grateful commitment is the basis and core of all true 'worship' (v. 1). It is the source for the Christian's 'renewed way of thinking', and the way we learn to 'discover the will of God' (v. 2).

Christian commitment has to be personal, but it is not private. It draws us into a company of people, who serve together and support one another in faith and fellowship. The church is 'one body in Christ' (v. 5). We need one another, we are meant to function as a team, in faith and humility (v. 3). As in any healthy body, the members bring different gifts and strengths. The gifts vary widely: teaching and caring, encouragement and leading (vv. 6–8). But the attitude in which we serve is the same whatever our gifts: love (vv. 9–10), energy (v. 11), steadiness of spirit (v. 12) and generosity (v. 13) are the lifeblood of the body of Christ.

Not that all is sweetness and light in the Christian service. Faith sometimes has to confront suspicion and opposition. The world can be a harsh and hurtful place, and at times the church has been too quick to copy that behaviour. But we are called to a very different way, to patience (v. 14), sensitivity (v. 15), gentleness (vv. 16–20), to the calm and determined practice of goodness, even in the face of evil (v. 21). Love is what we have to offer the world. We have discovered that love is infectious, for the love of Christ has been poured into our hearts (cf. 5:2). Now that love is to spill over, sometimes through the deliberate pouring out of our service and care, but even when we are jolted and disturbed it may still be goodness that overflows from us.

4   The state we live in   *Read Romans 13*

Romans 13 has been a controversial and disputed chapter. For it seems to give the Christian no leeway in the face of bad government. When the citizens of a country notice corruption in high places, or the exercise of totalitarian police powers, or war-mongering, or ethnic cleansing, are they simply to recall that 'the powers that be are ordained of God' (v. 1), and to assume that everything must be all right?

I think this passage warrants a more measured and discriminating response than that. In the time Paul wrote there was some unrest in Rome about taxes, an unrest so serious that the emperor eventually intervened to lighten the burden on the people. Paul tells his Roman readers not to withhold their tax payments, but to respect and honour the civil powers (vv. 6–7). Government is a gift of God. It exercises responsibility from God. So Christians should not ignore or avoid our duty to those who rule.

But dutiful submission is not at all the same thing as unquestioning approval. Our rulers are not perfect, but they are still called to promote justice and good conduct. They regularly need our prayers (1 Timothy 2:1–2), they sometimes need our criticism. It may at times be a Christian duty to remind a government of its God-given responsibility; indeed there is a long tradition of godly and candid criticism in the Old Testament prophets.

The Christian's submission, then, should not be blind, but should be perceptive and vigilant (v. 11). Our civil obedience is part of our love for our neighbour: it stands between 12:21 and 13:8, bracketed by our commitment to goodness and to love. We meet the debt of taxation as part of civil law, but also as an act of love for the people around us. And when the tax is paid, we still owe these neighbours the daily love of our hearts and deeds; only so can we follow the greater law, that comes from God and is fulfilled in Jesus Christ (vv. 8–10). So even if public life and the horizon of national and international affairs should be clouded by gloom, Christians may live as people of light (vv. 13–14), with one eye on the glory of God's coming dawn (vv. 11–12; cf. 8:18). That is our privilege, and part of our witness.

5 Unity in practice   *Read Romans 14:1—15:6*

Thus far the practical section of Romans has spoken of the Church as a united and interdependent community (12:1–13), and as a people called to live peaceably and loyally in the world (12:14—13:14). Now Paul moves on to tackle a delicate and important issue in the Roman Christian church, and perhaps an issue he has held in mind all through the letter. He is concerned for the unity of Jewish and Gentile Christians. In a number of places he has stressed that the gospel meets Jew and Gentile in equal ways, and sets them side by side before God (1:16; 2:9–10; 3:9, 29; 9:24; 10:12). He has shown how Israel's ancient story pointed to the coming of Christ (ch. 4), but has balanced that by explaining that the Jewish law is not an adequate alternative to the gospel (2:17–29; 7:7–25). He has had a double motive in view throughout: to help Gentile Christians to respect the Jews' heritage; and to give Jewish Christians the courage and determination to stick with their Christianity, even though most of the church in Rome has become Gentile.

So chapter 14 is about bearing the tension of Jew–Gentile differences in loving and patient Christian unity. Jewish believers had grown up avoiding certain meats. They would even avoid oil and wine, if there was any suspicion that a portion of the crop had been offered to a Greco-Roman god; for them, that would contaminate the whole consignment. So in practice many Jews would be rather abstemious, whereas many Gentile Christians would never have been so troubled by these anxieties. Paul tackles this issue at greater length in 1 Corinthians 8—10. Here he simply recognizes this division of outlook, and offers two pieces of practical advice.

First, Christians should understand that there are different views within the fellowship, and not compel one another into conformity (14:1–12). Second, they should be careful about their own conduct, and might even need to curb their freedom of conscience, for the sake of a sensitive neighbour (14:13–23). Food and drink are not at the heart of Christianity (v. 17), but if something as mundane as my eating and drinking disturbs another Christian's faith, then I should abstain (v. 21). Liberty of conscience does not always mean liberty of conduct. We are constrained by love, and by our belonging together in Christ, in order that we may be a people truly united in praise (15:5–6).

6 Tasks unfinished *Read Romans 15:7–33*

This passage has two themes—evangelism and ecumenism. The gospel is like butter: it is made for spreading; and when places it has been spread to are brought into contact, they ought to bond easily. Paul draws on a string of Old Testament scriptures (vv. 9–12), to back up his conviction that Jew and Gentile belong together. The hope of the Old Testament, the promise of the Messiah, was meant for the whole world (vv. 8–9).

So Paul's own missionary energies have been devoted to telling the nations about Israel's Christ, spreading the word out, drawing the peoples in (vv. 16–22). Indeed he regards the Christians in the Roman church as part of that world parish (vv. 15–16). Yet he is not content with looking back on a life's achievement, and conserving the churches already in existence. He has always tried to break new ground for the gospel (v. 20) and is keen to do so again (vv. 23–24). Evangelism is a never-ending task: it covers the whole breadth of the world and extends all through time. The Church of every generation has fresh duty and new opportunity, in sharing the gospel of Christ.

But the success of our evangelism is bound up with the quality of our Christian relationships. A badly fragmented Church loses some credibility and effectiveness in its witness. Paul had been passionate in claiming his freedom as a missionary, but he remained anxious to forge bonds of loyalty between his Gentile converts and the mother church in Jerusalem. He believed in unity (v. 7), he wanted the Gentiles to acknowledge a spiritual debt (v. 27), and he was concerned by reports of poverty among the Jerusalem Christians (v. 26). So he has gathered a gift of money from his Gentile congregations, and is preparing to take it to Jerusalem (vv. 26–28). He asks for the fervent prayers of his readers, that barriers of suspicion may be lowered, that the gift may be welcomed, and that he may be spared danger (vv. 30–31).

So as we leave Romans, Paul is eager to reach further shores and new faces with the Christian good news. But first he will invest time, energy and some risk in carrying a gift, a symbol of love, honour and recognition from one group of churches to another. Paul shows—and the church of every age is invited to take up—a steady commitment to evangelism and to Christian unity, for Christ's sake.

GUIDELINES

Romans has become known as a complex piece of theology, well suited for thinkers, for people who love to pore over their Bibles. But it is more than that, for it speaks with warmth and hope of the potential and power of the Christian life (ch. 8). It rejoices in the bonds and commitment that make up Christian community (ch. 12). And it leaves us looking forward: as the purposes of God unfold, we too are beckoned to take our part, by faithful Christian living, in the mission of God in the world.

> *Heavenly Father,*
> *as we follow in the footsteps of our forebears*
> *on our pilgrimage of faith,*
> *fill us with your heavenly grace*
> *and so make us faithful witnesses to all people*
> *of the love of Jesus.*

Grant that we, being firmly grounded in the truth of the gospel,
may be faithful to its teaching,
both in word and deed,
through Christ our Lord.

A pilgrim prayer used at Chester Cathedral.
Taken from M. Pawley, Prayers for Pilgrims, SPCK, 1991

For further reading

Here are three commentaries on Romans. The first two are solid, medium-length and clear. The third is much more thorough, extensive and detailed.

J.R.W. Stott, *The Message of Romans*, Inter-Varsity Press, 1994

J.A. Ziesler, *Paul's Letter to the Romans*, SCM Press, 1989

J.D.G. Dunn, *Word Biblical Commentary: Romans* (in 2 volumes), Word Books, 1988

On growing old

There is much variety in the situations of the elderly. And who can say, for that matter, when that venerable condition begins, let alone when it will end? It can certainly be a long and important part of a life. If there are hardly any biblical passages treating the matter at any length, at least there is much in the Bible to indicate the vital role, and indeed responsibility, of the aged. They are respected as wise, but responsible for bearing witness to the work of the Lord, handing on a crucial message to the next generation. Other aspects of old age appear in scripture, such as the propensity of the Lord to call and use the elderly in his special purposes. As we think together about some of the problems and privileges of later life, we shall therefore be able to read biblical passages in relation to our thoughts—and there is usually a lesson here also for younger readers! (No particular version of the Bible is required.)

22–28 JANUARY

1 Remembering   *Read Deuteronomy 8:1–11*

Very elderly Viv watched a lot of sport on TV. He had once been a referee, and would often shout, 'Send him off', at which Emma, the small black poodle beside him, would growl fiercely in agreement and shake her rag toy. So sport was a good subject for our long chats together—except that neither of us could recall the names of the great players we would allude to, and the harder we tried, the more the names receded. Yes, remembering becomes a problem as we get older, and yet how sharp and colourful were Viv's recollections of his early life in South Africa!

Remembering the past is something we can do with God's guidance, rather than at the whim of our own spirit. Nehemiah asked God himself to 'remember for good' (Nehemiah 13:31), and our own remembering is best done also 'for good'. So we remember the kindnesses of people, and bless them and thank

God for them. Resentments and grievances are best put away, forgotten, as God himself, in his new covenant, forgives, and remembers our sin no more (Jeremiah 31:34).

Above all, our remembering of the past should be a discerning of the way the Lord has led us, so that now we may know all the more that our life is all from him and for him. This is the great theme of our reading. Those who had been through the full forty years in the wilderness were now fairly elderly. Moses asked them, with the younger ones following on from them, to remember all the way which the Lord God had led them—with all the testing and humbling; and they were to see its meaning, namely that their life was sustained not by bread alone, but by all that the mouth of the Lord uttered. And if now they entered a rich land, with more comfort and pleasure, they must not forget the Lord their God and all the commandments and guiding words of his mouth.

Some of us in retirement enter a little promised land. Income may now be assured; our time may be more at our own disposal; we may move to a favoured place, and enjoy frequent holidays. Take care, beware, our reading would say to us also, lest we forget the Lord our God, and imagine our own hands have provided all this.

2   New challenges   *Read Jeremiah 1:4–10*

As our circumstances change, we face new challenges. Quite fundamental things may change in what was the pattern of our life for many years. Such changes may bring distress and dismay, but always there is opportunity. The Lord has not left us. He is still with us. What would he have us make of the new situation? There will be something special here that we can do for him. But often we are more aware of our limitations, and in this we are like the elderly Moses and the young Jeremiah. Moses was a very poor speaker, and said the Lord would do better to send some other person (Exodus 4:10–13); the Lord persevered with him, and this elderly person, 'slow of speech', became one of the world's greatest teachers.

In our reading, Jeremiah learns that he has been destined to speak for the Lord, and objects that he is too young to know how to speak. But again the Lord perseveres, and Jeremiah's service was to be of the utmost importance, a foreshadowing of our Lord's. God's words to him at his call apply to his servants of any age. First, we were born for a purpose——his purpose; so fundamental, that he 'knew' us before he began to form us in the womb. Such a purpose does not wear out; from beginning to end in this world, and beyond in the eternity of God, it gives a significance and value to our existence which no one and nothing can take away. Second, our response to his direction is a matter of trustful obedience; we go where he sends, speak what he commands, knowing that is for the best. Third, we need not fear, for he promises to be ever with us. 'I wouldn't go anywhere without him,' I heard an old lady say recently; and for his part, he promises 'I am with you to deliver you.' And fourth, he equips us for the task. Indeed we in ourselves have not the skills; but he will put into our mouth, our hand, our heart, all that is necessary.

The 'new challenges' in our changing situation may not be as evident to history as were those that came to Moses, Jeremiah, and indeed the ageing Abraham (Genesis 12:1–3), or in more recent times to Churchill, Adenauer and Mandela. But they will be significant enough if recognized as what our Lord wants from us, what we can offer for love of him, and what he will make part of his own mysterious and infinite work for the redemption of all his creatures.

3 The divine opportunity in weakness
Read 1 Corinthians 1:26–31

A fair-haired, dapper figure, Eric, 93, calmly pedals his tricycle through the congested traffic of the village to do his shopping, and parks where other vehicles fear to stay. He is organist for three churches, and the music of canticles and anthems is often of his own composition. When his playing was not required for a production of Roger Jones' musical 'Simeon', he happily joined the singers, and it was he who made and planted in the high bank outside the church a well-lettered board to advertise the production. Eric is but one example of elderly folk in our church fellowship who seem to go from strength to strength. Are they gifted with extra vitality of body and mind, making lesser mortals only more conscious of their frailties? If our portion is, by contrast, ever diminishing strength and extreme limitations of health, how can we serve God? His promise is indeed to be with us and to help us, but the big fact of our weakness, our incapacity, cannot be gainsaid.

In our reading, we are told that God actually chooses the weak, the lowly and the despised. Just as the cross itself may seem to the world to be weakness, foolishness, failure, and yet carries the fullness of God's power and wisdom, so he works through our weakness to set forth his glory. The pride of human strength is not so serviceable to him; but in the humility of our weakness is the divine opportunity.

And come to think of it, Eric does not appear as a superman; he just seems altogether focused on the tasks God has enabled him to do, living for his Lord in quiet humility. The apostle Paul would have all of us focused on Christ Jesus, as the One made by God to be all the strength we need—'our wisdom, righteousness, sanctification and redemption', or in other words, the One who has brought us back to God, to hold us there for ever. And Paul indeed would have us see the divine advantage of our infirmity, that the power of Christ may all the more rest upon us; God's word to Paul is for us also: 'My grace is sufficient for you, for my power is made perfect in weakness' (2 Corinthians 12:9).

4 The good old days *Read Psalm 145:1–12*

In his mid-eighties, Denzil is ever busy out of doors. In addition to tending his own little garden and those of indisposed neighbours, and on wet days doing carpentry in his shed, he keeps two allotments, which are a joy to behold. He has a great abundance of vegetables, fruit and flowers to give away, and calls on us regularly with a heavy bag. He likes to come and chat for over an hour, and shows that he is a keen observer of life, and gifted with a poetical eloquence, perhaps derived from his Celtic upbringing. He is not one to laud the past indiscriminately, but nevertheless the conclusion of many conversations is that in many respects the old days were better. The wood was well-seasoned, and the tools of better steel. The books were better bound and printed, and authors knew their subjects well. School discipline was salutary, and learning poetry by heart was beneficial. The gentry were courteous and considerate, and vicars had dignity and learning. Front doors were left unlocked, and some occupants even chided you if you knocked before entering. On all such matters, Denzil has illustrative stories, and will often bring an old book, magazine or cutting to reinforce his point.

It was a word from the Lord when Jeremiah told the people to 'stand at the crossroads and ask for the ancient paths, where the good way is, and walk in it, and find rest for your souls' (Jeremiah 6:16). These indeed were the good old ways—but, truth to tell, they had never been generally popular. They were ancient and good, reliable routes to find the soul's peace; but they were the ways of God's law, and of the heeding of his words. In the past, and still in the present, people have been inclined to follow their own devices. It falls to the elderly to commend, not the good old days of human merit, but the old days and ways of God.

Our reading is clear and beautiful. In the light of our reflections today, we should hear from it what it is that we are to extol and commend to the next generation. From the various phrases in these verses we must take to heart that our testimony of experience should be to the wonderful greatness and goodness of our Lord.

5 A calling to compassion *Read Ephesians 4:29—5:1*

Our friend, the aforesaid Denzil, includes the care of his neighbour Sharon's garden in his tasks, having sympathy for her heavy work in a senior nursing post, with long and unsocial hours; and he even goes to some trouble to fulfil her unusual wish that all her flowers should be white. Meanwhile, at our Parish Centre, another example of practical sympathy for the young can be witnessed every Tuesday: lunch and Talk Together is for young mothers and children, affording welcome change and relief and a chance to share the predicaments and pleasures of motherhood. The obvious success of this institution owes something to the fact that the strain of preparing and clearing up is inconspicuously eased by others, some of them in their eighties. They have knowledgeable sympathy for the stresses upon their young friends, and their kindness is shown with understanding.

With the diminishing powers and increasing ailments that accompany growing old, we are not surprisingly tempted to think ourselves deserving all the consideration. How wonderful it is, then, to see elderly folk who are full of compassion for the difficulties of the younger ones—for those anguished with problems that beset childhood, youth, and middle age. Their example teaches us to pray that we who are getting old may grow in consideration for the younger folk—practical consideration springing from tenderness and compassion.

The beautiful words of our reading fit well in the context of these thoughts. Let us avoid harsh and hurtful words, and pray ever that our words may impart grace, and serve to 'edify' or build up faith and courage in the hearers. We are then careful not to grieve the Holy Spirit, who is given us in pledge of our final redemption, and who especially watches over 'fellowship', the relationship of love that he would give us towards others. All bitterness and anger are to be put away, utterly displaced by tenderness and forgiveness, such as we ourselves experience from God in Christ. For the old, no less than the young, are summoned to imitate God and walk in love, as Christ loved us and gave himself up for us.

6 The valley on the way home *Read Psalm 23*

Of the two Cornish brothers, Ted had been up-country for many years, while Ernie still lived in the parental home. When they got together and were catching up with the news, their rather nasal and laconic conversation often fell into a pattern: 'Remember old so-and-so who used to…? Ah, well, he's gone on.' I think it was not so much that an unusually high number of their acquaintances were prone to 'go on', but that their going on was the most newsworthy occurrence. Still, it is true that as we get older, an ever higher proportion of our family and friends have left this earthly shore, and years come when they go on in rather quick succession. It is as though we are part of a generation that has come through a long journey overland, and is now close to the place of embark-ation, and it is not surprising that more and more of them are setting sail for that farther shore.

Our reading is perhaps the best loved of all the psalms. Its rich imagery has always something more to reveal to us. Above all, it testifies to the wonder of life with our Lord, a life beautiful in its peace and fruitfulness, but also in its eternal significance. How precious is that 'for thou art with me' (v. 4)! The 'valley of the shadow of death' is in itself a fearful place to walk through; any pilgrim, of any age, may come to it, but the old know of its closeness and inevitability. But knowing our Lord beside us, mighty and faithful, we shall fear no harm.

His kindness and faithful love are pictured as angels that closely attend us all the days of our life (v. 6)—and how often these 'angels' are known to us in good people, and indeed in animals! And who can say what comfort and help he grants us through the undying love of those who have gone on, and yet are not far away?

And so the inspired psalmist comes to his best thought of all: 'and I shall dwell in the house of the Lord for ever'. The Hebrew, however, more obviously means: 'and I shall return into the house of the Lord for ever', and perhaps the intention is: 'and I shall return (and dwell) in the house of the Lord for ever'. To keep this nuance, we might render: 'and I shall come home to the house of the Lord for ever'.

In this light, we see our earthly life as a going forth to places of hardship and danger, where, however, our good Lord has often refreshed us and given us many delights. And finally he goes with us through the last dark valley, his angels of Kindness and Love ever in attendance, until we are home again at last, to abide with him in joy for ever.

GUIDELINES

O God, whose power is made perfect in weakness, grant us such humility and love of your will that our life may still be a channel of your grace.

Inspire us to witness to the good old ways of your law, the ancient paths of your word, so that, in times when all exalt what is new, the truth of your salvation may ever gain disciples.

Needing consideration ourselves, may we by your grace be quick with consideration for others. May the fruit of our years be wise understanding and sympathy for the stresses borne by younger folk in this rapidly changing age.

O Lord, my Shepherd, through places rough or plain you have guided me. May I always know that you will not leave me, not even in the last valley, but will bring me home for ever.

Judges 9–16

In May and June 1998 we read Judges 1–8; now we continue from chapter 9 with the stories of Abimelech, Jephthah and Samson. With apologies to those who have retentive memories, I must repeat part of the introduction I wrote then and say that Judges is not one of the easiest books of the Bible for 21st-century consciences to read. It is not simply that it contains ruthless, barbaric and harrowing scenes, but that the author obviously has no qualms about making God the perpetrator of much of the violence he portrays. Those who decided that his book should be *sacred scripture* had no qualms either. This should remind us that here is an ancient book, author and religious community whose values are different from ours; and if we remember that there is much we can read in Judges with profit. There is another problem, however—the theology of the book. Judges works with the doctrine that goodness is rewarded and evil is punished. We know, just as other parts of the Bible also recognize, that things are not so simple in real life where the bad prosper and the good suffer every bit as much as the other way round. Therefore some dismiss this theology as simplistic. But I suggest that Judges is more subtle than this and that its theology points to some realities we would be unwise to ignore. We shall see.

The version used is the New Revised Standard Version (NRSV).

---

29 JANUARY–4 FEBRUARY   JUDGES 9:1—10:5

1   Abimelech   *Read Judges 9:1–6*

We join a long story part way through. Joshua-Kings tells the story of Israel from a bright beginning on the wrong side of the River Jordan into the Promised Land and then away to exile in Babylon. Its moral is simple—Israel are God's people and the tragedy is that they have brought the catastrophe of the exile on themselves. The story so far is that the Israelites have crossed the Jordan and conquered their way into the Promised Land. Canaanites aplenty remain, stubbornly defending their homeland and preventing the Israelites from occupying it completely. The Israelites settle here and there. Things go well when they do as God requires. When they do not, the Canaanites regain the upper hand. Oppressed Israelites then cry to the Lord who sends them leaders who free them from their enemies (the 'Judges' after whom the book is named). Things go well for a bit before going wrong again. So the cycle goes on.

Judges 8:22–23 and 29–35 set the scene for the story of Abimelech. Gideon (Jerubbaal) the hero—who had refused to let himself be made king after his successes against the Midianites—is dead and it is relapse time again. Baal-berith ('Covenant Lord') is the local god the Israelites are flirting with this time. Although there was a difference in status between marriage (a relationship between two free Israelites) and concubinage (between a free Israelite man and a slave woman), the children of both relationships were legitimate. Warning bells sound about Abimelech, in the word 'also' (v. 31).

Chapter 9 opens fatefully. Ignoring Gideon's stance, Abimelech plots to become king, a new departure in tribal Israel. His method of safeguarding his rule will be followed by later dynasts in Israel (1 Kings 15:29, 16:11; 2 Kings 10:1–11), as will his failure to do it thoroughly (2 Kings 11:1–3). 'Lords' (vv. 3 and 6) are simply 'men', 'leading men' or 'citizens' in other modern versions. The reference to 'one stone' in verse 5 suggests that he was making his slaughter into a sacrifice, but there is no reference anywhere to the God of Israel. The Lord's rule over them is quite forgotten (see 8:23). So much so that the Shechemites make Abimelech king at the very same sanctuary at which the Israelites had bound themselves in covenant to the Lord (Joshua 24, especially v. 26). That covenant is badly broken now.

2 Jotham's fable   *Read Judges 9:7–21*

Jotham, the other surviving son of Gideon, resorts to the only weapon he has—words; or, more accurately, satire. The city of Shechem stands in the pass between Mount Gerizim to the south and Mount Ebal to the north. Jotham climbs Gerizim to shout his message to the citizens below. His opening gambit looks as if he is still prepared to give them a chance, suggesting that if they listen to him and act on his words, God will listen to them and not regard their election of Abimelech as king as an act of rebellion (v. 7). By the end of his speech, however, when he flees to Beer (location unknown) to escape from his half-brother, it is obvious that he holds out no hope for them.

His satire is in two parts. The first is a joke about Abimelech. Three productive and useful trees decline the request from the trees to reign over the forest, but the bramble or 'thorn bush' in most modern versions—'bearing no fruit, giving no shade, yielding no timber; a useless and noxious cumberer of the ground' (G.F. Moore)—will agree to their request if it is made 'in good faith'. Then all the trees may rest in its shade. If, on the other hand, their request is not made 'in good faith', fire from the bramble will destroy even the mighty cedars. Abimelech is absurd and so are they for making him their king. But he is also dangerous and they are in danger from him.

The second part of his satire addresses the leaders of Shechem directly and turns on the word 'If' (twice in v. 16 and reiterated in v. 19). '*If* they have elected Abimelech in good faith'. Once posed, the absurdity of the question is obvious (v. 17). So with the warning that they will rue their choice ringing in their ears, Jotham flees.

3   An evil spirit from God   *Read Judges 9:22–25*

No one takes notice of Jotham and Abimelech rules for three years, but they are not three happy years. Nor would any reader of Judges expect them to be. 'You reap whatsoever you sow' is the message preached from chapter 1 onwards, and we know what it is that Abimelech has sown.

Verse 23 is difficult, especially if we forget that we are reading a story and begin to think too literally. The idea of God sending 'an evil spirit' is also found in 1 Samuel 16:14, 18:10 and 19:9 with reference to Saul's madness and similar to one in 1 Kings 22:21–23 which refers to God deluding Ahab's prophets. In the longer story we have met a God who 'hardened Pharaoh's heart'

(Exodus 10:1, etc) and who incited Sihon to resist so that he could punish him (Deuteronomy 2:30), as he will do later to David (2 Samuel 24:1). The key to understanding this lies in the Deuteronomic theology which underlies most of these passages—that actions have consequences, that we reap whatsoever we sow. Abimelech has sown violence and disorder, and he—with a little prompting from God, for there is no escaping the consequences of one's actions—is about to reap the same. This principle is woven into the warp and woof of life, our author believes, but occasionally God has to tweak a thread or two. The New Jerusalem Bible takes some of the difficulty away by translating the phrase as 'God sent a spirit of discord'.

Shechem stands at a strategic location where important routes from south to north and east to west cross. By robbing travellers on these routes are the Shechemites depriving Abimelech of his tax and customs revenue (v. 25)?

4   The end of Shechem   *Read Judges 9:26–45*

The antagonism between Abimelech and the leaders of Shechem intensifies. With the arrival of Gaal, about whom we know nothing, they see the chance to oust him. Gaal wins their confidence; perhaps he is something of a demagogue (though v. 28 is obscure and the translations vary). They celebrate 'in the temple of their god' (v. 27). Remember that this is Shechem, the site of Joshua's holy covenant (Joshua 24), a place in which solemn promises have been made which are not being kept. Under the influence of alcohol and religion, surely a dangerous combination (but a teetotal Methodist would say that, wouldn't he?), conspiracy is sown, boasts are made and believed.

But Abimelech still has support in the city, in the form of Zebul the governor, who sends him a report. He is now, presumably, back home on the family farm at Arumah (as in v. 41, although it is called Tormah in the Hebrew of v. 31). They devise a strategy. It works. Gaal just escapes with his life. Many of his supporters are not so lucky.

Verse 41 seems out of place, as the action continues the next day. Abimelech storms the city, kills all its inhabitants and razes it to the ground. It might have been a tactic to 'sow' a defeated area 'with salt' so that it was made permanently infertile and uninhabitable, but it is more likely that the expression simply denotes total destruction.

This destruction of Shechem prompts historical questions. Did it really happen? Can it be dated or proved? Such questions are inevitable and for some Old Testament scholars they are proper questions. These scholars read Judges as one of the 'Historical Books' and believe that, despite exaggeration and bias and all that kind of thing, these stories contain a kernel of fact. Others, equally faithful and committed, believe that such questions are misguided and that they are based on a misunderstanding of what kind of books Judges and its companions are. For these scholars, the question to ask is not, 'What happened?' but, 'What does this story mean?' For them, and for me, an archaeological expedition to check out this destruction of Shechem would be as pointless as looking for the remains of Noah's ark.

In the story, Jotham's warning has come true. They have reaped Abimelech's wrath. The bramble's fire has burned the cedars.

5   The end of Abimelech   *Read Judges 9:46–57*

The scene moves, according to NRSV, to a neighbouring town called 'Tower of Shechem' but the Hebrew is uncertain at a number of points. NJB calls the place Migdal-Shechem and leaves it unclear whether this is a separate town or the tower/citadel of Shechem itself, which is how GNB, REB and NIV understand it. The leading citizens, on hearing of the destruction of the nearby city, take refuge somewhere in the Temple dedicated to El-berith ('Covenant God'), another name for the Baal-berith ('Covenant Lord') of Judges 8:33. Quite where is another uncertainty: in its crypt according to NJB and REB, its tunnel according to NJPS (New Jewish Publication Society) and its stronghold according to NRSV, GNB and NIV. Abimelech, however, has done his military homework. He collects brushwood from a local hill (Mount Zalmon) and fires the place. There are no survivors.

Then he moves against Thebez, though no reason is given for an attack on this hitherto unmentioned place, and takes it as its inhabitants take refuge in its fortified tower. Abimelech proceeds with the same strategy as before, but is fatally wounded when a woman drops a millstone on his head. Too proud to die at a woman's hand, he asks his armour-bearer to finish him off. He killed his brothers 'on a stone' (vv. 5 and 18); now he is killed by a stone. God is not mocked, as Paul puts it in Galatians 6:7. Abimelech reaps what he has sown—note the 'repaid' of verse 56. As do the people of Shechem. Jotham's curse has done its work.

We have reached the end of the sad saga of Abimelech. As the long story unfolds the total loss of the northern kingdom, Israel, in 722BC and Judah's exile to Babylon in 597 and 586 will be blamed to a large extent on the nation's kings. The 'Deuteronomist' (the name we usually give to the author or group of authors responsible for Deuteronomy and Joshua—2 Kings) sets out rules for the kings (Deuteronomy 17:14–20) but it is not hard to see that he thinks even duly appointed kings are not a good idea. The Abimelech episode illustrates the damage that can be done when such power is taken by the wrong hands. A city is destroyed and hundreds or thousands die. Here is a warning indeed.

6 Interlude *Read Judges 10:1–5*

The circle turns. The evil brought about by Abimelech and the citizens of Shechem is neutralized from within as it were. Blessing is then restored through Tola who 'rose to deliver Israel' and subsequently maintained by him and Jair who between them 'judge' Israel for a total of forty-five years.

Tola and Jair are sometimes counted as 'minor judges' whose main responsibility was administering justice, but even here we see that the term 'judge' for these characters is somewhat misleading. Some English translations call them 'leaders' and 'chieftains' which are better terms for these charismatic heroes and guerrilla leaders whom God raises up to save his people. The thirty of everything in verse 4 simply denotes the kind of prosperity and success which are to be expected, at least in the Deuteronomist's theology, when people live by God's guidance (as also in Judges 12:14). Kings ride such donkeys (Zechariah 9:9). They can be used for carrying treasure or as ordinary working farmyard animals (Isaiah 30:6 and 24). 'Havvoth' means either 'villages' or possibly, 'tents' or 'encampments' (NJB) and Jair is the name of the legendary fighter who originally conquered them (Numbers 32:41). Note the other sign of prosperity in these verses—that these two judges 'died and were buried'. Their lives had reached their natural end and the proper formalities are observed. The contrast with Abimelech is nicely drawn.

GUIDELINES

Ideas about the early days of Israel are complex and controversial. For some scholars the Bible story tells it the way it was, beginning with Abraham and getting clearer as it goes. Others are much more cautious. What is increasingly widely agreed is that Israel as a people and an embryo nation came on the scene ('emerged' is the favourite word) around 1200BC. Major population growth and changes in the settlement patterns in the central highlands of Canaan around this time and accompanying social upheaval in the older city states in the region, which the historians observe, is not actually very different from the way the story is told in Judges.

My edition of the NRSV calls the book of Judges 'the story of a new community emerging from disparate groups that were trying to create an entirely new pattern of life… one in which all citizens had an equal range of opportunities. The Israelites rejected the absolutism of the Canaanite city states with their oppressive political and social systems… the creation of this new society was an immense struggle. In the midst of revolutionary social upheaval, the Israelites found support in their belief that they were ruled by the Lord who took the side of the lowly against their oppressors.'

The contrasting stories of Abimelech, who grasped at power, and Tola and Jair who were given it illustrate the conflict of ideology in ancient Israel. In the book of Judges Abimelech represents the values of 'Canaanite society' and Tola and Jair represent the authentic way in which Israel is to live. If Israel wants to live happily in the Promised Land—and such happy living is quite mundane and everyday as we see in the picture of it in Micah 4:4—they must do so by walking in the ways of the Lord.

So whether we think of how Israel is to live in the Promised Land after they have crossed the Jordan after the death of Moses, which is how the story is unfolding in Judges; or of how they are to live in the New Jerusalem and the New Israel when they return from their exile in Babylon, which is what the final editors have in mind, the choice is starkly simple. They either follow God's guidance or do what every other nation does. The choice is set out plainly as an either/or in Deuteronomy 30:15–20. That is the text for which the books of Joshua to 2 Kings are the sermon in which Judges 9:1—10:5 is one graphic illustration.

5–11 FEBRUARY   JUDGES 10:6—13:1

1 Prelude *Read Judges 10:6–18*

The cycle moves on. From peace and prosperity to trouble and oppression. This time the effect is felt in Gilead, which is today that part of Jordan east of the River Jordan and which had been so prosperous in the time of Jair. The West Bank territories in the south (Judah) and centre (Ephraim) suffer too (v. 9). The cause is the same as before: Israel 'did what was evil in the sight of the Lord' and in the same way as before (2:11–13; 3:7–8). They worshipped other local gods, six of which are mentioned and in so doing show that they do not appreciate what it is that God has done for them (vv. 11–13). Abandoning him they worship the Baals (or Baal) and the Astartes (or Astarte or the Ashtoreths or the Ashtaroth). Baal—'Lord' or 'Master'—is used in the plural or without a capital letter to refer to local gods, as here, but Baal was also the name of the Canaanite high god. Astarte (the Greek form of her name) or Ashtaroth (the Hebrew form) was one of the three chief Canaanite goddesses, her speciality being love and fertility. In the plural or without capital letters the word refers to local goddesses, as here. Although ancient and modern translations get quite muddled, the picture is plain enough: Israel is guilty of apostasy and, according to our author, the consequences are devastating. See the comment in this week's 'Guidelines'.

This passage does not hesitate to speak of God's emotions: his anger in verse 7, his petulance in verses 11–14 and that 'he could no longer bear to see them suffer' in verse 16. It is common, but quite wrong, to contrast God's 'anger' and his 'love' (and then worse still to think that the Old Testament describes the one and the New the other). As good parents get angry when their children hurt themselves and others and miss out on the good they have in them to be or become, so too God's anger is a sign of his love, not a contradiction of it. Whatever we make of this talk of God's 'emotions', however, it shows that he is not remote from or indifferent to his world and his people, but passionately involved with both.

2 Jephthah   *Read Judges 11:1–11*

As yet we do not know whether the Israelites' prayer of confession in 10:15 and subsequent act of repentance in 10:16 has been heard. Will the Lord deliver them or not? At first the signs are not good. The Ammonites mount another invasion of Gilead. The Israelite commanders do not look to God but look round for a military leader. The next character introduced into the story looks even worse than Abimelech. Though Jephthah is a 'mighty warrior' (as was Gideon in 6:12), he is the son of a prostitute rather than of a concubine, at odds with his brothers and supported by outlaws rather than kinsfolk. This is the one they seek out and send for. Neither is Jephthah's initial response to their request encouraging to them or to us. Is this another leader out to win power and all that goes with it for himself? Even the picture of the deputation of elders from Gilead is ambivalent. Do we admire them for their pragmatism in facing Jephthah's sneering question with the frank admission that circumstances alter cases? Or are they just like any other set of politicians who will change their principles as well as their policies the moment they become inconvenient?

That Jephthah might turn out to be very different from Abimelech begins to be a possibility in verse 9. He names the name of the Lord. Any fighting that is done, he insists, depends on the Lord for victory and not on the commander of the troops. The deputation, moved by his faith, swear an oath in the Lord's name. So Jephthah returns with them and in the sanctuary at Mizpah, confirms his commission before the Lord.

Finally a note about Jephthah's mother. Although we suspect that it is less his parentage than his success which threatens his half-brothers, it is his mother's profession which they use to exclude him. Jephthah's mother may be slighted by his half-brothers but no comment is passed about his father's role in his conception. The story of Judah and Tamar in Genesis 38:12–26 is a classic exposure of the same double standards around prostitution: it is OK for a man to use a prostitute, but not OK for a woman to be one.

3 Jephthah the negotiator *Read Judges 11:12–28*

Valiant warrior though he might be, Jephthah first attempts to negotiate with the king of Ammon, the only example of the use of diplomacy to resolve conflict in Judges. His point is quite simple and relies on a theology that he and the Ammonites share. In fact it was the common theology of the day, as we see in the inscription on the Moabite stone carved around 830BC on which King Mesha of Moab celebrated his victory over Israel. Chemosh, God of Moab, had given him victory over Israel, just as he had conceded victory to King Omri of Israel forty years previously because he was angry with his people. The belief was that a nation's god or gods fought for it and the fate of a nation lay with its god. 'So,' Jephthah suggests, 'why does the king of Ammon not accept that the Lord, the God of Israel, has given Israel this land which used to belong to the Amorites? It was never yours in the first place, so why are you trying to lay claim to it now? Why not simply make do with what your own god has allowed you to keep? Why tempt fate? After all, one's god does not necessarily guarantee one a victory, but sometimes permits his own people to be defeated in order to punish them...' This is exactly the same theology on which the book of Judges has been operating, as we have seen. Jephthah points out that the Lord gave victory to Israel over the Amorites, who had opposed them, but left Edom, Ammon and Moab, who had not, entirely alone. Thus the king should accept the will of his own god and leave Israel alone now (v. 27). If the King will not accept that, concludes Jephthah, we must see to whom the Lord will give the victory.

For the attitude of Edom (v. 17), see Numbers 20:14–21; for the defeat of King Sihon of the Amorites (vv. 19–23), see Numbers 21:21–32; and for the story of King Balak of Moab (v. 25), see Numbers 22–24. There is, however, an error in verse 24, for the god of the Ammonites is Milqom (or Molech), not Chemosh, who was the god of Moab.

4   The tragedy of Jephthah's daughter (1)
Read Judges 11:29–33

Verse 29 is encouraging. The 'spirit' or power of God comes upon Jephthah as it had on his predecessors Othniel (3:10) and Gideon (6:34). In that strength he advances on the Ammonites. So why does he make this fateful vow? He has already committed himself to the Lord and sealed that commitment in a solemn act of dedication (assuming that to be the meaning of verses 10–11). He has already told the Ammonite king that the outcome of their conflict is in the Lord's hands. Thus, against that background the vow can only be regarded as an act of faithlessness, a desperate attempt to guarantee the desired outcome by bribing God, an extra insurance against failure.

It also looks like an act of the most outrageous and inexcusable folly, though it is quite interesting to see how many commentators down the centuries have come to Jephthah's defence at this point. Even the NRSV footnote, in my edition, reads, 'Given the arrangement of homes with courtyards that housed domesticated animals, it is likely that Jephthah assumed that one of these animals would be encountered first upon his return home.' G.F. Moore dismissed that idea—and several more—splendidly in 1895: 'That a human victim is intended is, in fact, as plain as words can make it; the language is inapplicable to an animal, and a vow to offer the first sheep or goat that he comes across… is trivial to absurdity'.

Jephthah is deadly serious. This is no rash vow, but a carefully calculated and deliberate one. He is foolish, but worse than that, he is faithless.

The Lord, however, grants him the victory he seeks. If we ask how God works and acts in the world, as the Bible pictures him doing, verse 32 might be helpful. It says that Jephthah went out to fight and the Lord gave his enemies 'into his hand'. It appears that God cannot achieve anything by himself, that he needs the skill and willingness of a Jephthah. It appears too that Jephthah cannot succeed by his own skill and courage, that he needs the 'spirit' of God to empower him.

5 The tragedy of Jephthah's daughter (2)
Read Judges 11:34–40

Victory turns to tragedy as Jephthah's daughter comes out to meet him on his return. She, the nameless victim of her father's lack of trust in God, is then sacrificed to his refusal to try to sort it out with God (for 1 Samuel 14:43–45 shows that even vows can be renegotiated). Then Jephthah blames her. She has 'brought him low' and 'become the cause of great trouble to him' (v. 35)! She has actually done nothing at all. Whatever trouble he feels himself to be in is entirely of his own making. No wonder feminist interpreters of this passage have little difficulty in pointing to the patriarchal bias of the story. Whose tragedy is it, they ask— Jephthah's (because she is his only child and he is upset) or his daughter's? Perhaps it is because he knows this that he vents his anger with himself on his daughter.

Jephthah's daughter is remarkably calm about it all. Her sadness is that she will die childless and a virgin. Note how ideas change. In the understanding of ancient Israel she dies an unfulfilled woman. In the medieval church her virginity would be regarded as the highest possible state of womanhood. Today we would see her as a victim of a particular stereotyping which sees the fulfilment of womanhood in terms of being a wife and mother. And a contemporary narrator of her story would probably feel it necessary to slip in a warning to anyone who dared to offer any definition of what constituted fulfilment for a woman. And rightly so.

For the narrator, the story functions as an explanation of a particular custom, but there is no other reference to such a custom in the Old Testament. Attempts to link it with 'Canaanite fertility rites' of 'weeping for Tammuz' (Ezekiel 8:14) are forced. Likewise it is hard to see this story as a condemnation of human sacrifice, which was undoubtedly practised in ancient Israel before it was eventually outlawed (Leviticus 18:21 and 20:2).

The story is a double tragedy. First, the daughter dies because of her father's faithless folly. Second, her name is forgotten but her father is remembered as a hero (1 Samuel 12:11; Hebrews 11:32).

6 Tribal conflict and an interlude   Read Judges 12:1–15

We have met touchy Ephraimites in similar circumstances before (8:1). Jephthah lacks Gideon's way with words and this time fellow Israelites come to blows. The Gileadites are incensed by the insults hurled at them in the process, though verse 4 is too obscure for us to know exactly what it was the Ephraimites said. The Gileadites win and occupy the fords of the River Jordan, blocking the retreat of the fugitive Ephraimites. Identifying disguised enemies, however, is easy. Their dialect gives them away. 'Shibboleth' means either 'ear of corn' or 'flood' but any word beginning with *sh* would have done just as well. The numbers of Ephraimite dead are obviously excessive—there are more dead Ephraimites here than any other figure of dead enemies in the whole of the book of Judges except one (8:10) and more than in the tribal census figures given in Numbers 1:33 and 26:37. Biblical numbers are always difficult—from the great ages of the ancestors to the numbers of those crossing the Reed Sea or eating the bread and fish on a Galilean hillside. They only become a problem, however, if we want to read these stories as accurate historical or factual narratives and if we do that, the numbers are among the least of our problems.

There is no explicit connection in the story between this incident and the preceding tragedy of Jephthah's daughter. In each one, however, there is a connection between words and blood: Jephthah's vow and his daughter's sacrifice in the one and the Ephraimites' insults and their slaughter in the other. Is that perhaps why the summary of Jephthah's achievements in verse 7 sounds rather muted?

Three unknowns are listed in verses 8–15 who 'judge' Israel for a total of twenty-five years after Jephthah's death. This, added to the six years of his leadership, makes a total of thirty-three years of relative peace since the Israelites had cried to the Lord for help when they were oppressed by the Ammonites. As with Jair (see 10:3–5), their personal prosperity indicates the blessing of God on Israel at this time.

GUIDELINES

The issue raised in 2:11–13, 3:7–8 and 10:6–8 is a key one in Judges and in the Old Testament as a whole. 'You shall have no other gods beside me'—and woe-betide you if you do—is also the message of the first commandment (Exodus 20:2 and Deuteronomy 5:7) and of the Shema (Deuteronomy 6:4), both of which demand absolute allegiance to the Lord and the Lord alone.

It is not easy for some of us in our multi-faith world, particularly those who incline towards a pluralist understanding of religion, to appreciate this exclusive and hard-line stance towards other faiths and their gods. It is, at the same time, all too easy for some others to use this way of looking at things to justify ethnic cleansing and religious totalitarianism. Perhaps all of us need to accept that ideas in this area are as much open to change and subject to other influences as we saw in connection with the views on virginity and motherhood in 12:34–40.

To appreciate the reasons for the hard and exclusive line taken in Judges we need to remember that what was at stake, at least according to the Old Testament writers, was not simply the people of Israel's religious purity or theological correctness, but also their social morality and community values. The Deuteronomist, for example, believed that there was a battle going on for the soul of Israel, because with other gods came other world-views and value systems. We see this conflict of lifestyles and values perhaps clearest of all in the stories about Elijah in 1 Kings 17—2 Kings 2. Queen Jezebel and her religion sees nothing wrong with killing Naboth in order to acquire his vineyard. Elijah, on the other hand, believes that the God of Israel is one who defends the weak and upholds the rights of all. Baal and the other gods of Canaan, according to the Old Testament writers, do not value that social justice which is very near to the heart of Israel's vision of society. There is no doubt that to defend their ideology and theology they paint their pictures in the starkest of either/or terms, but for them they were in, literally, a life and death situation.

This is not how it seems to be for most readers of *Guidelines*, who live in a multi-faith, multi-ethnic and multi-cultural world in which tolerance and acceptance of diversity are key values. At the very least, however, it is no bad thing for us to be reminded by reading Judges that religion has consequences and that these consequences should be taken into account in evaluating the different religions currently on offer. Unlike today, the ancients in Israel did not believe that anything goes when it comes to one's faith and that of one's community, nor that religion was a harmless leisure pursuit which made no real difference to anything. We post-moderns might do well to pause to reflect on that.

12–18 FEBRUARY   JUDGES 13:1—16:31

1   Samson   *Read Judges 13:1–5*

The wheel turns. Now it is the Philistines alone who are God's agents of correction. For the next hundred years they will loom large in Israel's story. They were a Mediterranean people (part of the Sea Peoples as the Egyptians called them) expanding eastwards and arriving in Palestine (to which they eventually gave their name) just as Israel was emerging in the central highlands. Contrary to our use of the adjective 'philistine' they were both cultured and technologically advanced. As usual with the Old Testament's 'forty years' there is no need to count them for the phrase signifies a generation or so, long enough to forget what matters and to have to relearn it the hard way.

Verse 2 immediately gives a signal, for 'barren women'—the older the better—are always a sign that God is about to do something special. Such was the case with Sarah (Genesis 16–17) and Rebekah (Genesis 25:21) and so it will be with Hannah (1 Samuel 1–2): but unlike the others this one is not named. She is only 'Manoah's wife' or 'the woman'. The last woman we met in the story was, of course, Jephthah's daughter: young but a virgin and childless.

'The angel of the Lord'—last met when he appeared to Gideon in 6:11–22 (and previously in 2:1 and 5:23)—reappears. Old Testament 'angels' (or 'messengers', for that is what the Hebrew word means) are usually members of the 'heavenly host' sent to deliver a message; but they can be human 'messengers' such as prophets. The Israelites in 2:1, Gideon in 6:11f and Manoah in this incident do not at first see the angel to be anything other than a human messenger, but Manoah's wife has an inkling of her visitor's true identity (v. 6).

The message is that she will 'conceive and bear a son'. He will be *nazir*, 'consecrated to God'. Not, as usual, for a time but for life; even from conception, for his mother too must live under nazirite rules (see Numbers 6:1–21) until he is born.

Note the 'begin' in verse 5. A long struggle 'to save Israel' lies ahead which will not end until the time of David.

2   Manoah takes charge   *Read Judges 13:6–25*

The woman reports this meeting with an impressive prophet ('man of God') to her husband, omitting the bit about not cutting their future son's hair but adding that he will be a nazirite from birth 'to the day of his death'. Is the storyteller preparing us for something here?

What follows has a vein of comedy not far below the surface. Her husband—because he does not believe her?—asks God to send the prophet back with further instructions. When the angel returns the woman was 'sitting in a field' (?) and has to run to fetch her husband. When Manoah eventually repeats his question it is not answered. Instead the angel—knowing a little bit about women?—tells Manoah that 'the woman' must be very careful to do as she has been told.

Manoah offers their guest hospitality, and another clear link is being made here with the story of Abraham and Sarah and their visiting strangers (Genesis 18:1–15). This visitor, contrary to custom, declines to accept it or to tell Manoah his name. With what is happening slowly dawning on him, Manoah turns his meal into an offering as Gideon had done (6:19–24). All the modern translations except NIV and NJPS see a play on words in the Hebrew between the angel's reply and a title or description of God 'the Wonderworker' (NJB). What happens next confirms the messenger's true identity and the couple, like Gideon, are overcome with awe and fear. The common sense in the woman's reply contrasts beautifully with her husband's lack of it.

Verses 24–25 prepare us for the action which is to follow. She bears a son and names him. Sometimes our storyteller plays with the meanings of names of people or places (e.g. 1:26; 6:32) but mostly not, as here. The boy grows, blessed by God (is this a phrase which Luke picks up in 2:40 and 2:52?) As with his predecessors Samson is empowered by the 'spirit of the Lord' (3:10; 6:34; 11:29), though the verb translated as 'stir' or 'move' is only used elsewhere in the Old Testament about someone being 'troubled' by bad dreams.

3   Tate and Lyle   *Read Judges 14:1–20*

Although we know, more or less, when and why Judges was published, when and why the stories it uses were first told—and who first told them—is a matter of conjecture. Some of them, like the poem in chapter 5 are ancient and deadly serious, but some, like the stories of Samson have all the characteristics of an ancient 'tall tale'. We can imagine the regulars in the Spotted Camel chuckling at the jokes, shaking their heads over Samson's inability to understand women, laughing at the discomfiture of the Philistines and gasping at Samson's amazing strength as old Beniah tells the even older tale. It is a favourite. We can also picture the Deuteronomist toying with the idea of including this good old story in his book and deciding that, with a proper introduction (ch. 13) and a little comment here and there (as in v. 4) it would do nicely. Lighten things up. But serious, too.

Chapter 14 is not what we expect after chapter 13. Samson's behaviour as an adult hardly accords with someone living under the nazirite rule of life. Likewise there is something cheap about the way Samson uses the power from God which 'rushes on' him

(vv. 6 and 19; see also 15:10). None the less it is a rollicking tale which romps along.

Embedded in the story are a number of interesting glimpses of life in ancient Israel, not least of marriage customs. The marriage is an arranged one and first choice for a son's wife is someone from your own closer kin (v. 3 and as in the stories about the patriarchs in Genesis 24:1–9; 28:1–5). There is a stag night. Weddings require special dress and a best man. Samson's riddle is not, however, entertainment to enliven the reception. The word is used of the Queen of Sheba's hard questions to King Solomon (1 Kings 10:1), of the enigmatic sayings of prophets (Numbers 12:8; Psalm 78:2) and of the proverbs and allegories of the sages (Proverbs 1:6; Ezekiel 17:2). Though riddles can be a form of entertainment or reflection (Psalm 49:4) they can also be used to mock (Habakkuk 2:6), and that is how Samson asks his. Note too the antiquity and effectiveness of nagging. Sadly, we also see that racial abuse is age-old, for the 'uncircumcised Philistines' sneer (v. 3) was hardly coined by the author of our story.

4 Mayhem *Read Judges 15:1–20*

The drama (and the coarse humour) continues. When he has calmed down, Samson returns to Timnah with 'the ancient Near Eastern alternative to our box of chocolates', as one commentator puts it. Outraged by what he learns from his father-in-law, he takes out his anger on the locals. What are we to make of verse 3? Does it suggest that Samson has a conscience about his previous action? Or simply point us forward to more and greater violence to come? REB has 'jackals' instead of foxes in verse 4, taking up the suggestion that this action would be easier to carry out with jackals rather than foxes, jackals being common in Palestine and found in packs, whereas foxes are solitary animals and rare. The comic absurdity of the whole enterprise seems to be lost on commentators who resort to such explanations. The Philistines in turn take their vengeance on the poor woman and her father. Samson retaliates. The colloquial 'hip and thigh' of verse 8 becomes a 'sound and thorough thrashing' in NJPS. After that he hides. The Philistines come looking for him and his own countrymen hand him over to them. But that, too, is a ruse and leads to a spectacular slaughter followed by twenty years of peace.

Embedded in this tale are the usual explanations and sayings. The location of Lehi ('Jawbone')—mentioned elsewhere only at 2 Samuel 23:11—is unknown. Ramath-lehi means 'the Hill of Lehi' or 'the Hill of the Jawbone'. The rhyme in verse 16 can be translated in two different ways. One reads two identical Hebrew words with different meanings ('donkey/ass' and 'heap/mass/pile') in the first line of the verse, as in NRSV, RSV, and others, but best of all in NJPS:

> *With the jaw of an ass, mass upon mass,*
> *With the jaw of an ass, I have slain a thousand men.*

The other reads only the one Hebrew word ('donkey/ass'). This is preferred by REB and NIV which gives:

> *With a donkey's jawbone I have made donkeys of them,*
> *With a donkey's jawbone I have killed a thousand men.*

En-hakkore means 'the Spring of the Caller' (v. 19).

Verse 20 is repeated at 16:31 and is another of the Deuteronomist's comments inserted in the traditional tale he is using. We will consider it and Samson's character in general when we look at 16:31.

5 Samson and Delilah *Read Judges 16:1–22*

With the editorial note in 15:20 the years pass, the scene changes and the final episode of Samson's life begins. Attracted to a Philistine woman, as before, his night of pleasure ends with another demonstration of his strength in which he outwits the Philistines yet again. Gaza to Hebron is forty miles and that walk involves a climb of 3000 feet.

Samson's first two women have been unnamed. He had 'wanted' his first wife (14:3) and used the Philistine prostitute. The one he now 'falls in love with' is named, Delilah. The story makes no attempt to play with the name, though that has not stopped speculation about its meaning. Neither does it give her nationality. The story unfolds. As before, Samson gives in to persistent nagging (v. 16; see 14:17). Shorn of his seven plaits of hair (we have engravings of the ancient hero Gilgamesh which show him having six, three on either side of his face), Delilah hands him over to the Philistines. Eleven hundred pieces of silver makes it quite an easy thing to do (vv. 5 and 18). The Philistines take their revenge. But verse 22 opens up the possibility of another scene in the story as his hair begins to grow again.

Readers with short memories might be forgiven for forgetting that Samson was any kind of religious hero at all. He has certainly not behaved like one. Perhaps that is why the Deuteronomist slipped in his note in 15:20, to remind us that Samson was in fact one of the 'judges' or 'saviours' of Israel. Samson himself, however, had not forgotten. He had given the credit for his feat at Ramath-Lehi to the Lord, albeit as a justification for his churlish demand for a drink (15:18). Now he tells Delilah his secret, that, whatever his sexual morals may have been and no matter how much he may have been involved with foreign women, he is consecrated to God, a nazirite. It is interesting to note that neither in the ancient story itself, nor in the additional comments made by the Deutero-nomist, is any judgment passed on either of those two things, the latter of which is certainly seen as a failing in Joshua 23:12 and Deuteronomy 7:3.

6 Death in the temple of Dagon   *Read Judges 16:23–31*

Our raucous tale moves to its happy ending. A happy ending, that is, for Samson and the Israelites. Samson calls on the Lord for the second time, this time more politely but still primarily for his own sake rather than God's or Israel's. The title by which he addresses God in verse 28, 'Lord GOD' in NRSV, is the title 'Lord' (= Adonai) plus the special divine name (= 'Yahweh', probably). He dies a hero's death, taking a final vengeance on his enemies. The temple of the Philistine god, Dagon, whose statue had a human head and body and the tail of a fish, is destroyed and thousands with it. Do not puzzle over the architecture—trying to picture this temple and work out how those on its possibly flat roof could expect to see anything in the courtyard immediately below—just enjoy the story. Samson's body is retrieved by his brothers—so after his barren mother had given birth to Samson, she was obviously infertile no longer—and he is buried in the family grave. His life is over. He lies at rest.

Verse 31 is Samson's epitaph. He had 'judged Israel' for twenty years. Samson is not to be seen, the Deuteronomist insists, as a legendary strong man whose great strength was only matched by his folly with women and his love of a brawl, but as someone whose life and strength were used in the service of God and his purposes. Raised up by God when the people of Israel had suffered enough for their sins and on God's own initiative without the usual cry for help from Israel (13:1), for twenty years he had protected Israel from the Philistines, as the angel had promised (13:5). His death, which in the usual way of looking at things was a bad one because it was both untimely and painful, was actually a great victory in which he had further damaged the enemy. In his death, as in his life, Samson was different and odd and the stories about him can hardly be classified as edifying religious literature. Yet despite all of that, the Deuteronomist asserts, Samson could and should be numbered among the 'judges'.

GUIDELINES

When we read the Samson story we must not take it too seriously. It started life as a tale with a strong vein of rather coarse humour running through it. That, at heart, is what it remains. There is, however, a theological lesson to be learned from it.

The Samson story has attracted an enormous amount of interest from Old Testament scholars in recent years. Attention has been focused on it particularly as an excellent example of a storyteller's art and technique. The Samson story may be particularly instructive in that regard, but in its present setting it is more than a tale told and enjoyed in whatever settings in ancient Israel stories were told and enjoyed. It is a story included by the final editor or writer in a longer story and retold in that setting for a theological purpose. Thus, though we who read it for theological purposes can admire the technique and appreciate the finer points of the storyteller's craft it exhibits, and appreciate the narrative art in the story, that is not our only purpose in reading it. Just as it was not, if we may be so bold as to speak of the intentions of an ancient author or editor, the sole aim of the editor who included it—however admiringly—in his book.

The hero of the Samson story is the Old Testament's most unsavoury hero. No one can hold Samson up as an example of faithfulness and devotion to the Lord whose life and faith is to be a model for ours. Yet the Deuteronomist numbers him among the 'judges' through whom God's saving project was accomplished. At the very least this suggests that 'God is working his purpose out as year succeeds to year' as the hymn says, even if to some of us, the people he is using are not necessarily those with whom we might be comfortable. In fact, although Samson is the most unsavoury hero in the Old Testament, he is far from the only defective one. Many of its leading characters have faults and failings and moments of shame. Thus the Samson story is an encouragement as well as a good read. It helps us to see that in the end God's purposes will be achieved even if, in the meantime, he has to use flawed characters. Like Samson. Like me. Like you.

For further reading

G. Auld, *Joshua, Judges, Ruth*, Daily Study Bible, St Andrew Press

The Sunday of Forgiveness

In the Eastern Church the Sunday immediately before Lent is known as the 'Sunday of Forgiveness'. Before entering upon the Lenten fast Orthodox Christians direct their energy to mending broken relationships, to seeking forgiveness from God and their neighbour. They enter upon the way of the cross through the gate of reconciliation. For Anglicans familiar with the liturgy of the Book of Common Prayer, there will be echoes of the invitation to the confession in this call to amendment: 'Ye that do truly and earnestly repent you of your sins, and are in love and charity with your neighbours, and intend to live a new life…'

The selection of readings from Genesis over the next two weeks leads us into Lent in company with our Orthodox brethren. They trace a similar path, mindful of the words of Paul, 'If it is possible, so far as it depends on you, live peaceably with all' (Romans 12:18). In the abstract, forgiveness is easy to contemplate. In the particulars of our lives, however, it is more difficult to effect. But as these readings reveal, people have always been complex, and their motives often confused. We will encounter individuals scarred by a sense of failure, by anger and resentment. It is as it always has been. And in this we can take strange comfort. More importantly, we can also have courage and hope because these same individuals also encountered the graciousness and loving-kindness of God.

The translation used is the New Revised Standard Version.

19–25 FEBRUARY   TRUE HEROES

1 Shaming and blaming *Read Genesis 3:8–end*

It is difficult to read this ancient literature afresh. Familiarity with the text breeds in us not exactly contempt, but certainly complacency. We might anticipate an exploration of the questions which humankind periodically articulates about the phenomenon of existence: Is there a God? Whence is evil? If there is a God, where is he/she/it? In Genesis, however, the questions recorded are not ours at all, but God's.

For example, the first question is not, 'Where are you God?' but 'Where are you [Adam]?' The Garden of Eden is a story of humankind lost, confused, bewildered, estranged, and of God in search for them. Spiritual renewal begins when we hear that first question addressed to us personally, and own where we are in our lives before God.

Adam and Eve hid because they were afraid. Psychologists tell us that one of the most powerful of human emotions, some would claim the most powerful, is fear. What or whom we are afraid of will dictate how we behave, what we do or do not do. Is it coincidental that the phrase 'Do not be afraid' or 'Fear not' occurs in the Bible no less than 365 times?

God's second question to Adam is also interesting to ponder: 'Who told you that you were naked?' The subtext implied, but not stated, is '…because I [God] didn't'. Shame is different from guilt, but in practice difficult to distinguish. You can do something about guilt: make restitution, ask forgiveness. Shame is altogether more subtle and controlling an emotion. It lurks in the shadows of the shrubbery with Adam and Eve. When we experience these feelings we need to be cautious in our self-diagnosis. Feelings of guilt and shame can come from many places: our family, our upbringing, school, the church. Contrary to popular opinion, they are not infallible guides to our relationship with God.

Shame drove Adam and Eve to blame one another, and even God's creature, the serpent. This culture of shame and blame is as much the patterning of 'original sin' as anything else. It is certainly corrosive of human relating. It springs from our refusal to respond to God's invitation to life and companionship with him. In this context, God's question to Eve is significant: 'What is this that you have done?' God challenges us to take responsibility for our lives and actions. When we do so, we take the first step on the path of grace.

2   Am I my brother's keeper?   *Read Genesis 4:1–16*

Crime statistics confirm an unpalatable truth, namely that the majority of violence happens within the family. Ironically, the scriptures have always known this. The family is the primary locus of our growth and nurture: it is a place of love, acceptance and security. But it is also a place of conflict, competition, intrigue and sometimes, violence. Christian exhortation about family life and family values will carry greater weight in contemporary debate when it is also married to a more candid assessment of the reality and complexity of our human relating. And in this, as elsewhere, the scriptures are a faithful guide.

The sibling rivalry between Cain and his younger brother Abel is sometimes explained as evidence for an evolution in an ancient agricultural economy, with the triumph of the stable farmer over the itinerant shepherd. This may or may not be so, but it is incidental to the bitter reality of human jealousy which the story narrates. Why does God look less favourably upon Cain's offering? We are not told. Perhaps there is an implied criticism in that whereas Abel brought to God the 'firstlings of his flock' (v. 4), Cain brought merely 'an offering of the fruit of the ground' (v. 3). Thus God's comment to Cain, 'If you do well, will you not be accepted?' may indicate a defect of intention in the heart of Cain, rather than a failure to achieve.

'Let us go out to the field', says Cain to Abel. What makes Cain's violence worse is its premeditated nature. We are not dealing with an impulsive outburst of anger. Likewise his petulant reply to God's inquiry, 'Am I my brother's keeper?' when his crime is detected. There is a path that leads from disappointment and envy, to anger and resentment, and ultimately to violence and even murder, that weaves its way through the human heart. We need to know its route because potentially 'sin is lurking at the door' in each of us.

Finally, what are we to make of the mark of Cain (v. 15)? This is not so much a branding in punishment, as an act of divine protection. Just as God clothed Adam and Eve as they are expelled from Eden, so even in our crimes against each other, and our resultant wanderings, the love of God still accompanies us.

3   Endemic violence   *Read Genesis 6:9–22*

We tend to delight in the figure of Noah. Pictures of the ark and the rainbow, children's songs about the animals going into the ark 'two by two' are all fun. But in actual fact, the story of Noah and the flood is dark. It is a story of a corrupt world and endemic violence (vv. 11–13), and of a remnant that survives to start again.

In Christian circles discussion of sin tends to revolve around issues in personal relationships. These things are concrete and we relate to them readily. But they are not the whole picture. The scriptures paint a broader canvas, describing the corporate nature of sin, a reality bigger than individual moral failure. Societies and their structures need constant renewal and reformation because they degenerate, become corrupt, and propagate injustice. Injustice in turn breeds anger and resentment, and this can spill over into violence.

Furthermore, as the story of Adam and Eve illustrated, our readiness to blame others when magnified as a corporate phenomenon results in groups and minorities being made scapegoats. Ultimately it fuels the drive to ethnic cleansing. National psyches can become diseased as both the scriptures and more recent history teach us. It is against such corporate madness that the prophets will rage and deliver their message of the righteousness of God. Nations, and not just individuals, will come under judgment.

In these dark times how is the person of faith to respond? To assume responsibility for all the mistakes and crimes of one's generation is a sure recipe for mental illness. The figure of Noah, however, offers a different model of church as saving remnant. Sometimes in the tide of human affairs, 'when the earth is corrupt and full of violence', the role of the Church may be to withdraw from engagement, to have no truck with evil, to be an ark of safety for the vulnerable, and to batten down the hatches when the flood-waters rise. Thus we will need to pray 'to discern the signs of the times' (Matthew 16:3). We will also need to scan the horizon for rainbows (v. 13), signs of God's faithfulness, and hang onto them. Such signs give us the stamina to persevere and to survive when the skies are dark.

4 Marital stress *Read Genesis 16:1–16*

Abraham and Sarah (or Abram and Sarai as they are called here) provide us with a powerful insight into the pain of a childless marriage. In the course of the story, the more clearly God's promises were spelt out to Abram, the more clearly Sarai saw herself as a failure. Although his legal wife, and although managing the household with skill, Sarai felt keenly the humiliation of her infertility. Each year that passed diminished her hopes of becoming pregnant, and giving to her husband the child of God's promise. In her despair she may even have come to the mistaken conclusion that she had for some reason forfeited God's favour.

It is at this point that Hagar, Sarai's Egyptian slave-girl, enters the story. In ancient societies various avenues were open to a childless couple, including adoption and surrogacy. Sarai's suggestion to Abram that he might father a child through Hagar was a socially acceptable convention. What Sarai had not anticipated (perhaps naively) was the emotional upheaval such an arrangement would generate. It is clear that the pregnancy gave the slave-girl a status and pride which no amount of social convention would crush out of her.

Sarai's misery leads her to remonstrate with Abram: 'May the wrong done to me be on you!' (v. 5). In retrospect it was to become clear that Sarai's attempt to remedy her childlessness had not been part of God's plan. But we can all be wise after an event. Sarai instinctively blames Abram for the situation they were in rather than admit that she had been the originator of the idea that had back-fired. But what was particularly reprehensible was that she used her position of authority over the girl to wreak her vengeance, treating her spitefully.

Hagar runs away and makes for home. Shur was the eastern district of Egypt, and the road to it across the Nile Delta must have been lonely. The text suggests that there was only one spring where drinking water could be found, and there 'the angel of the Lord found her' (v. 7). Once again it is God who does the seeking and the questioning. He invites Hagar to share the reasons for her journey. Although God asks her to return to Sarai (which must have been a hard thing to contemplate), there is a courtesy and tenderness about this divine encounter that is moving. As the name of her future son, Ishmael (meaning 'God hears') signifies, God does indeed listen to our cries of anguish.

5 Sibling rivalry   *Read Genesis 21:1–21*

Originally, it had been the intention of Sarah (as she is now called) to adopt Hagar's child as her own, but this did not happen. Perhaps such a scenario became a psychological impossibility once the two women had clashed so violently; and with the birth of a son to Sarah herself, things changed dramatically.

As all parents know, introducing a new baby into the home of an existing brother or sister is a tricky business. The child can feel unwanted and supplanted by the new arrival. Thus perhaps it was predictable that Ishmael, who for some years had been the centre of attention, should feel displaced and jealous at the arrival of his half-brother Isaac. Isaac may have been as old as three by the time of his weaning. In ancient society where infant mortality was high, the event merited a real celebration because to have survived thus far was a good indication that the child was strong and healthy.

It is not clear from the text what was going on between the two boys. The Hebrew can be variously translated as 'mocking' or 'poking fun'. The NRSV adopts the more neutral verb 'playing' (v. 9). The verb puns on the name Isaac in Hebrew. Whatever was happening, Sarah interprets Ishmael's behaviour negatively, and demands that Abraham expel the boy and his mother. Although Abraham is distressed by his wife's outrageous demand, he complies, and the two boys are separated. Isaac was to be God's chosen instrument because he was the child of promise, a theme which Paul takes up as an allegory, contrasting salvation by human effort and salvation by faith (Galatians 4:21–31).

The story of Hagar's dismissal is a horrible episode. The abandonment of the child by his mother who cannot face the prospect of her child dying from dehydration makes for painful reading. But in the face of such tragedy God reveals himself as One who hears our cries—this time, literally the crying of a child—and redeems the situation.

6 The binding of Isaac   *Read Genesis 22:1–19*

As with many episodes in scripture, the binding of Isaac (to give it its proper title) has been interpreted in various ways.

Anthropologists suggest that the story was told to enshrine the divine prohibition against child sacrifice in the Hebrew community. This was certainly something that distinguished the Hebrews from their Near Eastern contemporaries. But there are other resonances we should note.

In the story of Abraham this episode was undoubtedly his greatest test. Indeed, so painful was it that he did not even tell his wife. There is a loneliness about the figure of Abraham as he sets out with his son for the land of Moriah. The threefold repetition of the divine command (v. 2) to offer up as a burnt offering 'your son, your only son Isaac, whom you love' leaves no room for manoeuvre.

Hebrew worship was normally accompanied by animal sacrifice, so there was nothing out of the ordinary in his movements to have merited attention. And yet why is God requiring Abraham to sacrifice the very child whom he himself had promised to this ageing couple? What sort of a God is this? Capricious, to say the least. In the event, at the last minute, the divine voice intervenes to save the child: 'Do not lay your hand on the boy or do anything to him; for now I know that you fear God, since you have not withheld your son, your only son, from me' (v. 12). Christians have found in this language, and in the substitution of a lamb for sacrifice, imagery with which to speak of the significance of the sacrifice of Christ. But for the present we must allow the story to stand in its own integrity, and ask what it is about.

It is conceivable that what this story alludes to is what happens when the parent–child relationship gets distorted. It shows us in dramatic form what happens when we invest our children not simply with unrealistic expectations, but with divine expectations. Isaac was the child of promise, the gift of God to an ageing couple. But the gift had become their possession and (unknowingly) their god. They worshipped their child. That is why Abraham had to be challenged to him go.

GUIDELINES

We have been challenged this week not to view the heroes and characters described in these stories from Genesis through rose-tinted spectacles. Instead we have allowed them to emerge as they truly are: uncertain, confused, vulnerable and insecure people, some of whom are deeply flawed. And yet it is through these same persons that God is able to work his saving purposes for humankind. If God can use them, can he not use us? Verses from the orthodox hymn for the 'Sunday of Forgiveness', the Sunday before Lent, are haunting with their refrain and plea for mercy.

> *Banished from the joys of Paradise,*
> *Adam sat outside and wept,*
> *and beating his hands upon his face, he said:*
> *'I am fallen, in your compassion have mercy on me.'*
>
> *O Paradise, share in the sorrow of your master*
> *who is brought to poverty,*
> *And with the sound of your leaves pray to the Creator*
> *that he may not keep your gate closed for ever.*
> *'I am fallen, in your compassion have mercy on me.'*

If the encounters and stories we have studied have sometimes witnessed to the sordid reality of sin, they have also witnessed to the providence of God and his redeeming love. We have glimpsed the paradox and triumph of grace, and have just cause for hope.

---

26 FEBRUARY–4 MARCH   TRUE RECONCILIATION

1   Jacob and Esau   *Read Genesis 25:19–34*

Rebekah's twins were neither identical, nor friends. Sibling rivalry was apparent from the moment they emerged struggling from their mother's womb, with apparently Jacob's hand clinging to his elder brother's heel. Rebekah had had a difficult pregnancy with violent movements of the two children in her womb, prefiguring their rivalry in life.

Ancient Near Eastern custom gave special status to the eldest male child who on his father's death received a double share of the inheritance and became head of the family. Isaac's liking for his outdoor, hunter son augmented Esau's already privileged position as first-born. Jacob, by contrast, is a mummy's boy: quiet, reserved, staying at home. He was an opportunist, scheming and manipulative. He was also Rebekah's favourite. All the ingredients for family conflict are in place.

As is invariably the case in Hebrew, names are significant. 'Esau' sounds like the Hebrew for 'hairy'. We are told that as he emerged from his mother's womb, he appeared red (v. 24), presumably because he was covered with blood. He sells his birthright under oath in a moment of impetuous stupidity for a stew of lentils ('that red stuff', v. 30) to stave off his hunger. This, we are told, was the origin of his nickname Edom, meaning 'red'. The name 'Jacob' is equally nuanced. It means 'he supplants' or 'deceives'. The Hebrew for 'heel' and 'to take by the heel' or 'supplant' has the same consonants, hence the play on words. But earlier (Egyptian) versions of the name Jacob mean 'May God protect'. As the story of Jacob unfurls, both meanings will have significance.

Neither Jacob nor Esau appears an ideal candidate for becoming heir to the covenant promises of God. The family appears in many ways dysfunctional. And yet these are the flawed persons that God uses for his purposes of love. Each of them will experience transformation, healing and forgiveness, but not without considerable personal pain. When we turn to our own lives and stories, and reflect upon our upbringing and families, our rivalries and petty jealousies, there is always room for hope.

2   The deception   *Read Genesis 27:1–29*

There can be few things more difficult to carry to the grave than the knowledge that one has deceived one's own father. This was the burden that Jacob was to bear throughout his life.

The scriptures paint a picture of an old, enfeebled Isaac, blinded by cataracts, totally dependent on his wife and children. Although he was to live for many more years yet (see Genesis 35:27–29), his vulnerability must have exacerbated his preoccupation with death. Anxious to settle things while he still had some energy, he seeks to give Esau his blessing. And yet there is duplicity even in this. First, Isaac invites only Esau to the ceremony, deliberately excluding Jacob. And second, he endeavours to keep the transaction secret, though as with any 'last will and testament' it relied on witnesses for its legality. What Isaac had not reckoned with, however, was the scheming of his wife, Rebekah.

It is clear from the scriptures that although Isaac and Rebekah are still married, they had long since gone their separate ways. At some point in their marriage, love died. In its place grew animosity and recrimination. They used their children as pawns to score points off each other. If Jacob may be criticized for his manipulative scheming, it is something he learnt from his parents. Rebekah's scheme was fraught with danger. But so deep was her antagonism to her husband, and so strong her lust to see her favourite son succeed to the inheritance, that she was prepared to take the consequences of failure upon herself (v. 13). In the end, Rebekah did bear a terrible price for her scheming because she never saw her beloved Jacob again.

Jacob goes through with the deception, though twice he has to tell his father a direct lie, even to the point of claiming the assistance of God in catching good game! Isaac appears somewhat gullible. Perhaps like his elder son Esau, Isaac's love of good food could cloud his judgment. And so Jacob receives the blessing, in confirmation of the birthright his elder brother had surrendered to him so casually.

This story throws into relief the ambiguities of our own motives, and how easily we justify deceiving others, but end up deceiving ourselves. Perhaps our prayer should be that of the psalmist: 'You desire truth in the inward being: therefore teach me wisdom in my secret heart' (Psalm 51:6).

3 The rejection of Esau *Read Genesis* 27:30–45

The return of Esau from his hunting expedition, preparing the savoury game stew his father loved, and finally bringing it to Isaac with a request for his paternal blessing, is a haunting story, full of pain. The bitter cry of Esau, 'Father, bless me also' (v. 34), is poignant. It still has the capacity to ring in our ears as it must have done in Isaac's. Jacob's deception is unmasked, and the grief of Esau knows no bounds (v. 38). The silence of Isaac himself adds further poignancy to Esau's misery.

Despite the cruel trickery of Jacob the blessing remained his, and with it the best of the grazing land! Esau is directed by his father to other territory and another destiny, to a life of virtual exile, 'living by his sword' (v. 40), presumably as some sort of mercenary. Doubtless, such fighting became a channel for his pent-up anger, hurt and frustration, and became its own solace. For the present, his murderous hatred of Jacob is hardly surprising. Upon Rebekah's advice Jacob flees to Haran, to stay with her family until Esau's anger cools and it is safe for him to return. In the event, Jacob was to stay away twenty years, and Rebekah dies without ever seeing him again. We are told that Esau had already taken two Hittite wives (Genesis 26:34–5) neither of whom were pleasing to his parents. It was one of the few things they could agree on! So Rebekah's plan for Jacob to seek a more suitable wife among her own people found the ready support of Isaac. This becomes the rationale for Jacob's escape, and the context of his own redemption.

The parting of Jacob and Esau raises many questions for us, not least how we deal with disappointment in life. How do we cope when the future we had been led to envisage is suddenly taken away from us? There is a real bereavement to be negotiated. Then there is the issue of deception. How do we cope with feelings of betrayal? Words of the psalmist come to mind: 'It is not enemies who taunt me—I could bear that; it is not adversaries who deal insolently with me—I could hide from them. But it is you, my equal, my companion, my familiar friend with whom I kept pleasant company' (Psalm 55:12–14).

4 The return of Jacob *Read Genesis 32:1–21*

Twenty years in our narrative have passed. During those years much in Jacob's life has changed. He has acquired two wives, children, numerous servants and possessions, cattle and livestock. He has also suffered the ignominy of being himself deceived by his future father-in-law, who tricked him into marrying Leah as well as Rachel whom he loved. The experience, and his hard labour to win the hand of his beloved, combined to work its own purification in him.

Jacob now returns home, not only a wealthy man but also a wiser one. On the journey he hears news that his brother Esau is on his way to meet him, with some four hundred men (v. 7). Evidently, Esau had also met with success in his own life. Even after all those years, Jacob still instinctively falls back into old patterns of fear of his older brother. Anticipating vengeance, he divides the household and retainers into two companies for safety. He also devises a strategy for placating his brother. He sends ahead droves of sheep, goats, camels and cows as gifts for his brother by way of restitution. It was a laudable strategy. But what is more significant are his words, 'I am not worthy' (v. 10). It was Jacob's first admission of guilt, no doubt intensified by a sense of the precariousness of his position, but also emerging out of a profound sense of God's graciousness to him. His prayer to God for safety is as intense as it is sincere, and it emerges from a man who has (at last) learnt the value of integrity.

5 Wrestling with God   *Read Genesis 32:22–32*

It is night. Jacob is left alone by the river Jabbok, his household having gone ahead of him. Now in his solitude, he is confronted with the ghosts of childhood and his deepest fear—the wrath of his brother Esau. And yet apparently Jacob is not alone, because 'a man wrestled with him' (v. 25) until dawn. The stranger eventually overpowers Jacob, but only by dislocating Jacob's hip. In spite of the terrible pain he must have been in, Jacob persists in clinging to the stranger, refusing to release him until he reveal his identity and bless him.

The stranger refuses to reveal his identity. Instead he names Jacob 'Israel' because, he said, 'you have striven with God and with humans and have prevailed' (v. 28). Compare our earlier discussion of the significance of Jacob's name (see Monday's notes on Genesis 25:19–34). Jacob names the place by the river Peniel, literally meaning 'the face of God' because he said, 'I have seen God face to face and yet my life is preserved' (v. 30).

This extraordinary episode has engaged the religious imagination across the centuries. It was the stimulus for Wesley's great hymn, 'Come, O thou traveller unknown'. One of the paradoxes running through the scriptures is that, on the one hand, no mortal can see God and live. And yet on the other hand, the vision of God is our destiny and its fulfilment. In the psalms we are often encouraged 'to seek God's face' (e.g. Psalm 27:8). In the Gospels, Jesus says that the pure in heart shall be blessed because 'they shall see God' (Matthew 5:8).

Thus in Jacob's wrestling with God we have an image of our engagement with the divine. Prayer is not a cosy chat with a tame God, but an encounter with an unknown God who refuses to be our prisoner or puppet. From such an encounter we will emerge changed, and perhaps (and this is the most difficult thing to contemplate) like Jacob, limping. We shall emerge healed of our fears. As Jacob discovered, if he had striven with God and prevailed, what could man do to him?

6   The reconciliation of the brothers   *Read Genesis 33:1–11*

So powerful is the story of Jacob wrestling with God at the ford of the Jabbok that people tend to stop there, and never reach the climax of the story, and discover what happened when the two brothers did eventually meet. The arrival of an armed bodyguard must have been hugely intimidating to Jacob. After all, his was only a family group, devoid of armed protection. Not surprisingly, therefore, Jacob is cautious, anxious to protect his wives and children. But his encounter with God at Peniel had transformed him. This time he goes ahead of the company to meet Esau alone, seven times prostrating himself before his brother in contrition for the past.

We are told that Esau ran to meet Jacob, embraced him and fell on his neck, and that they both wept (v. 4). Reconciliation was effected. All the bitterness of the past, the recriminations, the jealousy and spitefulness were swept away in an embrace of mutual forgiveness. Fear has been cast out by love. Jacob's generosity to his brother, tokens of goodwill and restitution for past wrongs, are rendered superfluous. Esau has all he needs and more.

In their conversation, one of Jacob's comments stands out. 'Truly to see your face is like seeing the face of God' (v. 10). Jacob's words are not cheap flattery. Coming in the wake of his experience at Peniel, they signal a conversion of real significance. At Peniel, Jacob wrestled with God and prevailed. He had seen the face of God and survived. Now, for the first time, he is able to recognize in his estranged brother the face of the same God. As St Antony of Egypt was to put centuries later, 'Our life and our death is in our neighbour'.

GUIDELINES

The story of Jacob and Esau is one of the most extraordinary in the whole Bible. It is remarkable for the candour with which it describes their relationship. It is sometimes said that the trouble about burying the hatchet is that you always know where you have buried it. Reconciliation in their case was a long and fraught business, and immensely costly. The story also witnesses to the unpalatable truth that wisdom invariably comes through pain, and not in spite of it.

Perhaps this prayer of Evelyn Underhill is worth making our own this Lent:

O Lord, penetrate those murky corners
where we hide memories and tendencies
on which we do not care to look,
but which we will not disinter
and yield freely up to you,
that you may purify and transmute them:
the persistent buried grudge,
the half-acknowledged enmity
which is still smouldering;
the bitterness of that loss
we have not turned into sacrifice.
We bring all these to you, Lord,
and we review them with shame and penitence
in your steadfast light.

*If you enjoy your Guidelines
Bible reading notes, why not consider
giving a gift subscription to a friend
or a member of your family?*

*You will find a gift subscription order form
on page 157.*

Ecclesiastes

Ecclesiastes is one of the 'Wisdom Books', along with Proverbs and Job. Their writers are more like theologians or philosophers than other Old Testament authors. Now there are theologians and philosophers who are good at raising questions, and others who are good at providing answers. Proverbs belongs more in the second category, Job and Ecclesiastes more in the first. David Hubbard, former President of the seminary where I teach, put it this way: 'Proverbs says, "These are the rules for life. Try them and you will find that they work." Job and Ecclesiastes say, "We did, and they don't."' Proverbs offers us ground rules for understanding life. Job and Ecclesiastes help us to live with experiences that belie the ground rules.

In Ecclesiastes, Solomon is a test case for discussing how far we can find answers to the big theological and philosophical questions, though it never uses Solomon's name. This in itself hints that we are not to take the allusion to Solomon literally. The same applies to the Talmudic rabbi's description of Solomon as writing the Song of Songs with the enthusiasm of youth, Proverbs with the wisdom of maturity, and Ecclesiastes with the disillusion of old age.

Ecclesiastes' language is more like the Hebrew of New Testament times and afterwards than any other parts of the Old Testament. The word for a garden in 2:5, for instance, is *pardes*, which comes from the Persian word from which we get the word Paradise (in the Old Testament it otherwise comes only once in Nehemiah and once in the Song of Songs). This itself suggests that Ecclesiastes may be one of the later books in the Old Testament. But dating matters less with Ecclesiastes than it does with some other parts of scripture. Its questions are timeless.

I use the New Revised Standard Version.

1   The pointlessness of rushing around
Read Ecclesiastes 1:1–11

The author(s) of this book put their reflections on life on the lips of one they call *qohelet*, which NRSV and NIV translate 'Teacher'. The word comes from *qahal*, an assembly or congregation. The word Ecclesiastes ('churchman') itself comes from the Greek word for an assembly, so that gets it right. The theology in this book is the kind that raises more questions than it provides answers, but it is proper 'church' teaching, not some kind of exercise in destructiveness.

I live in a society characterized by a relentless activism. Christians as much as anyone else spend their lives rushing around ceaselessly on the freeway and never stop doing business on their cell-phones. 'What do they gain from it all?', Ecclesiastes asks. Relentlessly they pursue new experiences—new music, new films, new fashions, new holiday destinations. 'The eye is not satisfied with seeing, or the ear filled with hearing', Ecclesiastes observes. If in due course they collapse in front of the television, the adverts inexorably promise them something new—a new car, a new hamburger, a new computer, an 'all-new episode' of the series that follows. But 'there is nothing new under the sun', Ecclesiastes comments. Their society through no fault of its own has no past, though it longs for one, and it has no way of knowing what it might look like in the future. 'The people of long ago are not remembered, nor will there be any remembrance of things to come', Ecclesiastes reflects.

Southern California is the society where Western civilization is tested to destruction, so the rest of the West had better pay attention to how the experiment is going. The West in general lives by the myth of progress. Because technology advances, therefore humanity has progressed. Now I am grateful for the invention of the flush toilet and mains sewage, but it is hard for us to acknowledge that in most areas that matter, humanity has made no progress over the millennia. Ecclesiastes offers to deliver us from our self-deception.

2 The futility of research and self-indulgence
Read Ecclesiastes 1:12—2:11

The person behind this book is not only a 'churchman' but a son of David and king in Jerusalem. Israel of course had only one person who was traditionally thought of as its great philosopher-king, David's immediate successor, Solomon. His reputation makes him the ideal person to imagine undertaking the investigation that concerns this book. He was the original Southern Californian. He tried everything. He can testify from experience concerning matters that ordinary people can only speculate about. In addition, he had the reputation as the great philosopher. He thought as well as acted. That, too, should enable him to reflect on human experience in an instructive way.

1:12–18 constitutes an introduction to his testimony, summarizing the results of his great experiment. He confirms the claim of 1:2–11, and specifically confirms that our vast human activism cannot achieve things that matter or put right the real problems of the world (1:15). The country that can put a man on the moon cannot solve the problems of poverty, prejudice and inequality in its back yard. The society that puts huge emphasis on research into psychological and social problems cannot enable people to find happiness. The logical result is to be quite disillusioned with the notion of research.

2:1–11 then reports on Solomon's experiment with pleasure in particular. Now if there is a society that has tested pleasure to destruction, it is also the land of Los Angeles, Hollywood and Disneyland. It drinks fine Californian wines and watches countless comedy programmes on television and in the cinema. It is one of the music capitals of the world and one of the sex capitals of the world. It has built fine houses and museums, planted thousands of fruit trees, and constructed monumental irrigation systems. It attracts cheap labour from countries around the world. It comprises half of a state that has an economy greater than that of most of the actual countries in the world. And it is a deeply and widely unhappy society, which proves the truth of the testimony of Solomon without acknowledging the fact to itself.

3 So what shall we do? *Read Ecclesiastes 2:12–26*

Solomon's great experiment does not make him conclude that research, work and relaxation are pointless. They are indeed *absolutely* pointless, but they are nevertheless *relatively* worthwhile. They cannot provide ultimate answers or fulfilment, but they can provide something.

One of the foundations of modernity was the attempt to discover ultimate answers by starting from scratch rather than from supposed 'divine revelation'. Descartes thus began from 'I think, therefore I am'. But the subsequent history of thought has established that philosophy cannot generate answers to ultimate questions. In that sense, wisdom is useless. But wisdom still excels folly as light excels darkness (v. 13). It is *absolutely* useless but *relatively* useful.

One way we seek to find meaning is through work, but our work is also *ultimately* meaningless. Who knows how our successors will carry it on, whether they will ignore it or undo it or prove it wrong? Second-hand bookshops and university library stacks are full of the dusty, now-unread writings of 19th-century biblical scholars, and the works upon which I labour will soon join them. But our work is *relatively* useful. Perhaps my writing these notes may help someone see how Ecclesiastes impacts on their life. That is not nothing.

So in a moment I can break for lunch and rejoice in what I have done this morning (v. 24a). It is a gift of God that I can do that (v. 24b), and this is perhaps one reason why I can rejoice in it. We cannot start from ourselves and reach the conviction that God is there. But if we start from the conviction that God is there, that changes the way we look at our lives and the little things that give meaning to them. And the conviction that God is there and is the source of life's little pleasures is as reasonable a conviction as Descartes's 'I think'. God has not given us the answers to the big questions, but God has not given us nothing.

Straight after that little encouragement, however, Solomon pulls it back. Even our capacity for those little enjoyments is qualified by an awareness that there is a randomness about who receives them (v. 26). Ecclesiastes will not let us turn little answers into the big answer.

4 For everything there is a time   *Read Ecclesiastes 3:1–15*

The book abandons Solomon's imagined testimony and moves in a new direction. Different experiences and activities all have their time. The passage speaks of very different kinds of experiences and activities. On one hand, birth and death are events we have no control over. They happen to us; we do not make them happen. The first expression literally means 'a time for giving birth' (AV margin), which suggests a more solemn contrast. Weeping and laughing, mourning and dancing are also experiences built into life. We have no control over the events that provoke them.

In contrast, human discernment and decision-making are involved in planting and uprooting, in demolishing and building, in throwing away or collecting stones (which might be connected with building, but the expressions are a puzzle). The same is true of embracing and refraining from embracing, gestures that suggest entering into friendship and making commitments. It is true of seeking and giving up for lost, keeping and throwing away. It is true of tearing your garments in mourning and repairing them to begin normal life again, and it is true of silence and speaking. It is true of love and hate—in other words, of war and peacemaking. This last pair may also help us to understand the statement that there is a time to kill (the word means 'slay') as well as a time to heal. If 'a time for birthing' means 'a time for being born', perhaps this denotes 'a time for being slain and a time for being healed'.

There are thus uncertainties about the details of this poem, but what about the whole? When the Byrds made it a top ten hit in the 1960s, the idea that there was an appropriate or necessary time for life's activities and experiences presumably came across as a comfort. Ecclesiastes' subsequent comments about times in verse 9–15 fit with that, though they qualify it in a way consistent with 'Solomon's' testimony. Yes, all these human experiences have their time. But what is the framework in which they all fit? God has not told us. It is a clearly postmodern point in a quintessentially postmodern book. We cannot know the nature of the big picture into which everything fits. But perceiving the nature of the little pictures that make up life is not to be despised.

5   In the place of justice, there is wickedness
Read Ecclesiastes 3:16—4:3

Like the Torah, the Wisdom books interweave theology and ethics. If Ecclesiastes is going to agonize about existential questions, then, they will include ethical ones. Why is there so much injustice in the world? Ecclesiastes was as familiar as we are with a world in which people like him and us are able to control the rules by which society and economics and politics and the law work. Without doing anything illegal, the rich get richer and the poor get poorer. The rich own their land (or their home), eat well, and provide for retirement. The poor do not. In the community of faith (Israel or the Church) there ought to be 'justice and righteousness'. We could paraphrase these as 'power and authority exercised in a way that reflects the rights of people who are bound up together by mutual commitment, like people in a family'. Instead there is 'wickedness, wickedness'. We could paraphrase that as behaviour that ignores the way we are bound together. So what attitude do we take to that?

Suppose we look forward to a day when God will judge everyone (3:17). While there have been occasions when God has intervened in Israel's life in this way, there have been long periods when God has not, and the intervention that may come one day is little use for people who are dying today. If we affirm the conviction that God will undertake a great judgment at the End, there is no empirical evidence for that, and no teaching in Israel's tradition about this either. Ecclesiastes likes being empirical, starting from what we can know. What we know is that everyone dies, human beings as well as animals. What happens afterwards is speculation (3:18–21).

While he then comes back to his regular practical solution, that we should enjoy what we do have (3:22), he follows that with a more gloomy alternative perspective. Our human inhumanity to one another is indeed overwhelming. People who have not been born and have therefore not yet witnessed it are more fortunate than those who have (4:1–3).

6 The advantages of companionship; the perils of religion
Read Ecclesiastes 4:4—5:7

The attempt to achieve is an inherently lone venture. We are seeking to make our mark, to do better than the next man. I use the gender-specific language advisedly, because in our culture this has usually been a male affair. The same seems to have been true of Ecclesiastes' culture. Ecclesiastes' exhortation is one that in our culture women have more often instinctively lived by, though they have now been able to join the rat race. The book urges that collaborative work is better than individual work. Admittedly its argument is very down-to-earth in the advantages it sees in two people working together (4:10–12a). Three people working together is even better (4:12b).

Ecclesiastes is also down-to-earth in the insight he offers on religion. His first warning corresponds to one that recurs in the prophets. A well-to-do person, at least, is able to do just the right thing by way of sacrifices, but this may not be accompanied by the kind of life that God approves outside the temple. It is wiser to listen to what prophets, priests, and philosopher/ethicists have to say (5:1). The Torah itself was never interested in sacrifice unaccompanied by right living.

Second, the Psalter is full of praises to sing and protests to utter, some going on at great length. Ecclesiastes believes we need to set the awareness of God's awesomeness alongside the awareness of God's approachability (5:2–3). We might compare the stress on reverence and awe in Hebrews 12 with the stress on childlike freedom in Romans 8.

Third, both the Torah and the Psalms also assume that people often make promises to God, but Ecclesiastes wants people to think before they pledge. Don't make a promise you are not prepared to fulfil (5:4–6). This might be a special danger at a moment of great enthusiasm in worship, or of great personal need.

Fourth, the development of apocalypses such as Daniel reflects the way God can guide through dreams. Ecclesiastes joins with a prophet such as Jeremiah who emphasizes the way in which dreams that allegedly come from God may actually come from people's own imaginations (5:7). How the sentence works is obscure, but the punch line is clear: 'have reverence for God'. Translations tend to render this phrase 'fear God', but Ecclesiastes no more wants people to be afraid of God than other Old or New Testament writers do.

GUIDELINES

What is the significance of this extraordinary book? Here are some possibilities to consider:

• *Is it a statement of the darkness into which the gospel came? It has been used in evangelistic Bible Studies to help people face the reality of life without Christ.*

• *Is it an essentially positive book—one that first portrays the nature of the darkness, and then shines out with light?*

• *Is it a book that gives believers permission to face hard questions? We do not have to avoid these, even if we cannot always answer them very well.*

• *Is it a book that actually urges believers to face hard questions, rather than pretending that we have all the answers?*

• *Is it a book that simply acknowledges the contradictoriness of life and faith, and leaves us with it?*

Which makes sense of your own reading of the book and of you yourself, in the light of what it is and what you are?

12–18 MARCH **ECCLESIASTES 5:8—12:14**

1 **The best things in life are free?** *Read Ecclesiastes 5:8—6:9*

One of Ecclesiastes' recurrent themes is money. It acknowledges that money is really important, but urges that it is less important than people think.

• *It is strangely deceptive, or strangely unfulfilling (5:10). A current television advert acknowledges that the most precious things in life are priceless, but for all the rest we have a certain* credit card. We decline to acknowledge that more money and things will do us no good (cf. 6:7–9). And as a result, we are inhibited from enabling some poor people (for whom a little more could make a huge difference) to have that little more.

- *Increased wealth never seems to go as far as you think it will (5:11). The cost of acquiring it has to be offset against the gain from it.*

- *Increased wealth brings anxiety with it. An ordinary working man may not have much, but he has enough, and he does not have to worry about how the stock market is faring (5:12).*

- *This wealth is always precarious. You can never be sure you will make the right decision about when to buy and when to sell (5:13–14a). You can make a bad decision and end up with nothing, which is hard in itself, but even harder when you put so much effort into making your money in the first place instead of (say) lying on the beach (5:14b–16).*

- *Or your affairs may collapse through no fault of your own, or death may deprive you of the chance to enjoy them (6:1–6). Then your anger and frustration can make you much more unhappy than the person who never had what you lost (5:17).*

We have to sit loose to money, and a starting point is acknowledging what Ecclesiastes says. The sensible thing is to enjoy the good things of life that God gives, without pretending that they can provide ultimate satisfaction or meaning. Once more, they are not everything, but they are not nothing (5:18–20).

2 Facing human limitations *Read Ecclesiastes 7:1–7, 23–29*

Call no one happy till they are dead, said the Athenian statesman and philosopher, Solon. Only then can you make a definitive judgment. Death is a good thing, then, because it makes a definitive judgment possible (7:1). The comment reminds us how temporary our reputations can be, and how provisional our judgments must be.

We are going to die. It is a fact that we work hard to avoid. Ecclesiastes believes that it has decisive importance for the life we live before death. Keeping aware of where we are bound helps us make happier decisions now. Only a fool forgets that (7:2–4). It is but one facet of the fool's unreliability (7:5–7).

Again Ecclesiastes reminds us that his conclusions have limited significance (7:23–25). Here he seems to be reverting to giving 'Solomon's' testimony about what he has discovered. This is supported by the introduction of another reference to the 'Teacher' in verse 27, the first since 1:12. That may point to part of the explanation for what follows.

Verses 26–29 seem extraordinarily misogynistic, and puzzlingly so. How could their author go on to write 9:9? Indeed, verse 29 (which suggests that all human beings fail) looks in tension with verse 28 (which suggests an exception to that rule). Further, 'man' in verse 28 (*adam*) is actually the word for a human being, the word that recurs in verse 29. This underlines the problem.

Three possibilities may help us with the text. First, if 'Solomon' speaks again, the thousand women are the ones mentioned in 1 Kings 11:3, whom he indeed allowed to lead him astray. The warning is then couched as a warning about women, but ironically so, because it is as much a warning to men about themselves. Second, an implication would be that if this is one man's warning testimony about the mess one can get into with women (a warning about our capacities as men!), then it invites a responsive formulation in which women reflect on the way men can be 'bitter as death'. Third, Roland Murphy among other commentators neatly undoes the problem by changing the punctuation of verse 28: 'What my mind has sought repeatedly, but I have not found, is that 'one human being among a thousand I found, but a woman among all these I have not found'. This statement is one Ecclesiastes goes on to disagree with. Men are not even one-tenth of a per cent better than women. All have perverted their way. It is an even gloomier conclusion, worthy of Ecclesiastes.

3   Facing the facts about death   *Read Ecclesiastes 9:1–12*

Here are the facts, then. First, death comes to everyone (9:1–3, 11–12). God is the one who gives life and the one who eventually takes it back, but we can see no rationale about how God does that.

The righteous and wicked, the clean and polluted, the good and evil, the religious and the irreligious, the wise and the mad, the people who take oaths and the people who refrain from this: they all die. Belonging to the first group ought to make some difference: maybe you should live longer. But both groups are in God's hand, and how and when you die seems to be a matter of whim.

Second, death means your human experience is all over (9:4–6, 10b). You have no hope. While you are alive, you may still have prospects. When you are dead, you have none. Nothing will ever again happen to you. Death means no knowing, no reward, no being remembered, no loving, no hating, no jealousy, no acting, no thinking.

Ecclesiastes presupposes some practical facts about death that are common to Old Testament thinking as a whole. They overlap with death as we experience it, though not as we always think about it. Old Testament faith assumes that what happens to the body is a guide to what happens to the person. This is a natural assumption if you believe that the body is a true expression of the person, but the hold of Greek thinking on Christian faith often makes us assume that the body does not really matter.

When a person dies, the life visibly disappears from them. They cannot move, act, laugh, cry, or worship. If the body cannot do these things, it is hardly conceivable that the person (the 'soul') can do so. Being human is too bodily for that. We await the resurrection of our bodies so we can do these things again. But Ecclesiastes had no basis for believing in such resurrection, and insists on being rigorously empirical and not consoling us with pie in the sky when you die.

It is precisely against the background of the fact of death that Ecclesiastes invites his audience to affirm life (9:7–10a). The fact that it is all we have is reason for enjoying it, not for devaluing it.

4 Attitudes to the king *Read Ecclesiastes 9:13—10:20*

In Egypt, teaching of the kind that we have in the Old Testament Wisdom books was collected to form a resource for the education of people who would work in the civil service. Both Proverbs and Ecclesiastes include material on how to relate to the king, and this might form a natural part of wisdom for someone involved with the royal court. Ecclesiastes' material on the subject reflects his characteristic hard-nosed stance.

First, an ordinary person with insight may fulfil a role that is actually more important than the king's, but ordinary people are unlikely to be remembered for that (9:13–18). One senses that Ecclesiastes would rather be the ordinary person with insight than the person who merely has position and power. It is another sign that Ecclesiastes is hardly to be identified with Solomon in real life.

Second, you need to be able to keep cool if you work at court (10:4). As long as the king stops short of 'off with his head', keeping cool will probably be your salvation.

Third, on the other hand Ecclesiastes is a political and social conservative and believes in the proper order of things (10:5–7). There are people who belong to the ruling class and people who belong to the ruled, and both should stay in their place. Otherwise chaos rules (cf. 10:16–17).

Fourth, you need discretion if you are to survive (10:20). It is amazing how rulers sometimes get to know things.

The material on kingship is not very coherent and thus mirrors the nature of Ecclesiastes as a whole. One of the perceptive commentators on the book, Michael V. Fox, has written about *Qohelet and His Contradictions* (Sheffield, 1989). It is one of the glories of Ecclesiastes not to oversimplify things. Both the theoretical questions about life, and the practical ones, are complicated.

5   **Remember your Creator in the days of your youth**
                                   Read Ecclesiastes 11:7—12:7

The contradictoriness of Ecclesiastes continues in this last section of the concrete teaching in the book. On the one hand, we are to enjoy our lives. As young people we are to rejoice in our youth, as old people we are to rejoice in the number of years we are given, and we are to 'think positive'. Yet we are also to keep in mind that youth yields to old age, life yields to death, the length of life is far exceeded by the time we spend dead, and in old age continuing life can become more a burden than a privilege.

12:1–7 constitutes a profound conclusion to Ecclesiastes' treatment of death, though a puzzling one. The puzzlement and the profundity issue from its combining several pictures, which interweave literal description and imagery to convey the loss that old age and death involve.

The first image is that of fading light and a gathering storm (12:2). The picture of old age begins with an equivalent to our talk of the autumn of our lives. The image reverses the process in Genesis 1 whereby God brings light into being and sets sun, moon and stars in the sky. In old age, a person may have more and more difficulty seeing the light, and at death these lights go out for the individual.

The second image is a great house gradually falling into disrepair and disuse (12:3–4). Its staff and its inhabitants are getting older and incapable. The house has lost its place as a centre of life and activity in the community. The silence of death has descended upon it.

Third, the passage pictures an old man losing his faculties. Initially it speaks more literally (12:5a), though it complicates this by describing his deterioration by means of a number of figures (12:5b). One way or another the passage describes the increasing weakness of old age.

Finally the passage portrays the arrival of death itself (12:6–7). It does this first in figures and then in theological language that again sees death as a reversing of God's acts of creation, when God shaped the first man's body from dirt and breathed life into it. The life-breath disappears and the body dissolves.

Ecclesiastes is not wrong. There may be more to be said about what happens after we die, but that can only be said after we have accepted the facts that Ecclesiastes urges.

6 The value of a goad   *Read Ecclesiastes 12:8–14*

The book closes where it began, only more so. 'Vanity of vanities', it repeats from 1:2. The expression forms a bracket round its teaching. 'Vanity' (*hebel*) is one of Ecclesiastes' favourite words. He is responsible for half its appearances in the Old Testament. Literally it means a breath or a breeze, but it is usually used figuratively to denote something that has no substance. It is often applied to images of gods, which have no substance and are useless and empty. The repetition of the word suggests 'utter emptiness', 'utter futility'. The conviction from which the book starts is that life goes nowhere and history manifests no progress, and this fact makes human life look quite empty. The conviction with which it closes is that the fact of death carries the same implications.

The last paragraph of the book then closes in the third person, so that 12:9–14 pairs with 1:1. Whoever wrote or compiled the material in 1:2—12:8 with that summarizing bracket around it, the opening and close of the book are someone else's comments. In his study of the way different books of the Old Testament are 'shaped to function' as canon, *An Introduction to the Old Testament as Scripture*, Brevard S. Childs has particular success with Ecclesiastes. He shows how these opening and closing words invite readers into a balanced attitude to this book as these words take it on its journey towards becoming scripture.

On one hand, we have noted that these comments begin by calling the writer 'churchman'. They now repeat the term, and add that what we have been reading is indeed the work of a 'wise man'. This is a theological term in the Old Testament, not a merely academic one. These are words of truth, well-taught (12:10). The summary goes on to a brilliant encapsulation of how this wise man's teachings work. They are like goads (12:11). They hurt you, they make you say 'Ouch', but they do that in order to drive you forward. Once the kind of thing that Ecclesiastes says is out there, it cannot be unsaid.

On the other hand, enough is enough (12:12). One Ecclesiastes in the canon is a good idea. A canon full of Ecclesiasteses would not be. The reader needs to keep in mind the basic convictions of wisdom and to set Ecclesiastes in its context (12:13). The fact that there is no empirical evidence for some statements of faith does not mean they are not true (12:14).

GUIDELINES

As I write these notes, my wife is lying on the settee at the other end of the room, to safeguard against her getting pressure sores.

She has multiple sclerosis. Twenty years ago, she worked as a psychiatrist. Just last week we had a Christmas card from one of her psychotherapy patients, who remembers the sessions she had with Ann and looks back on them as a decisive shaping influence on her life. Today Ann cannot remember what country she lives in, nor what day it is, nor what are the names of the two carers who have shared in looking after her for over two years, nor what is the name of the grandson who brought her such joy when he was here a few weeks ago. She is virtually unable to swallow (she eats via a feeding tube) or to speak. She is watching the television news, though I am not sure how much she takes in. On that news we have been hearing of the terrible cost of the Russian invasion of Chechnya, of the suffering of the local people and of the Russian bodies surrounding their tanks. The pictures were too grim to show us. In a moment I will take her out for a walk in her wheel-chair in the warm January sun, and we will have an ice-cream, and if we are lucky she will be able to eat a little of it, and as I push her back up the hill to our apartment I will sing silly songs and pre-tend I am not going to make it to the top, and she will laugh. It is not enough, but it is not nothing, and it is certainly not to be despised. It is a gift from God. That is what Ecclesiastes says. It is also a wonderful gift from God that this book should be in the canon of scripture. I cannot imagine how it got through some community screening procedure. Actually I can. I do not think they were fooled by the reference to Solomon. I think they were overcome by the truth it speaks.

For further reading

Robert Davidson, *Ecclesiastes and Song of Solomon*, St Andrew Press, 1986

Wesley J. Fuerst, *The Five Scrolls*, Cambridge, 1975

Roland Murphy, *Ecclesiastes*, Word Books, 1992

R. N. Whybray, *Ecclesiastes*, Sheffield, 1989

The Gospel of Matthew
Chapters 19–28

In our previous readings of Matthew's Gospel, most of the events in the Gospel have been located in the Galilean area. Here in chapter 19, the action moves from Galilee onto the road to Jerusalem, as Jesus moves towards his death and resurrection. The closer Jesus gets to his fate, the closer the kingdom of God draws near. Jesus therefore instructs his disciples about life under the kingship of God, pointing out the differences between life now and life as it will be when the kingdom is realized on earth.

19–25 MARCH   **MATTHEW 19:1—21:45**

---

1   Along the road to Jerusalem   *Read Matthew 19:1–15*

Although Jesus' ministry in Galilee has ended, and he has now turned towards his final goal of death on the cross, he continues to treat the crowd with compassion and heal their sick. Predictably, the Pharisees again confront him, and continue their debate of his teachings. Their sustained opposition foreshadows the hostility Jesus will meet from the religious authorities in Jerusalem.

Again Jesus stresses the absolute righteousness of the kingdom of God and its expected ethics, a code of behaviour whose righteousness exceeds that of any teaching by the current religious authorities. In his answer, Jesus refers to the original creation story of Genesis, a time of perfection before the fall from grace of Eden's inhabitants. The kingdom of God that Jesus teaches is a renewal of this original state of perfection: before the fall, a provision for divorce within the Garden of Eden would have been unnecessary. Therefore, no divorce would be allowed—nor would it be necessary—in the perfection of the new kingdom of God.

Having laid out the ideal standard of the approaching kingdom of heaven, Jesus then moves to illustrate the ideal standard of those who would gain entry to the kingdom. At the beginning of chapter 18, Jesus made it clear to the disciples that only those who become humble like children would enter the kingdom of God. Here we receive a reminder of those words, as Jesus orders the disciples that the children who were brought to him should not be hindered from meeting him.

Children stand as the model for the faith and conduct of the disciples. By example, they teach the adult followers of Jesus what it means to be humble, faithful and 'least' in the kingdom that Jesus speaks of. To be child-like is to be innocent of the problems that come with riches and status, and therefore more receptive to the message of God.

Though the ideal of the kingdom of heaven and its attendant righteousness is always before the disciples of Jesus, nonetheless they continue to fall short of its requirements in the present interim era. Elsewhere in his Gospel, Matthew makes it clear that the full dawning of the kingdom on earth will not happen until the return of the Son of man at the last day. At that time, the earth will be cleansed of evil and sin and the righteous will inherit the world in the perfect state that God intended it to be.

2   Riches and righteousness   *Read Matthew 19:16–30*

The model of child-like innocence now gives way to the story of a young man whose riches prevented him from making a full commitment to the life of discipleship. Jesus' encounter with the rich young man leads to his pronouncement on the dangers of wealth and the contrast with the rewards of sacrificial discipleship. Though the kingdom of God demands one's total commitment and the acceptance of personal sacrifice, the rewards more than compensate for the large cost involved.

The young man who approaches Jesus has already received all the religious and moral instruction that he needs. In answer to his question in regard to acquiring eternal life, Jesus says that one more thing is required of him—to give up all his great riches with the proceeds going to the poor. The young man cannot do this, as he was more attached to his possessions than to following God in the radical way that Jesus advocated. His love for neighbour did not extend to the sharing of his wealth.

Back in chapter 6, Jesus had already made it clear that a disciple could not serve both God and money (6:24). Our previous readings of Matthew have shown that Jesus had a lot to say regarding wealth and poverty. He warned people not to store up treasures on earth. He reminded the disciples that he himself had no home or possessions. He ate with the poor and marginalized. He told a rich man to give away all his possessions to the poor and followed this by announcing it would be easier for a camel to go through the eye of a needle than for a rich man to enter heaven. This story of the rich man shows us the true heart of Jesus' ministry. Loving one's neighbour was about sharing wealth with the poor of the community. Following God was about dedicating one's life to the kingdom, and preoccupation with God's business, not the business of accumulating riches or possessions.

Today, those of us who live in the so-called First World must beware of becoming like the rich man. We cannot sidestep or ignore the serious warning that Jesus makes here in regard to wealth. In living as disciples, we must not compromise in our commitment to God or neglect to live in such a way that allows the vision of the kingdom for justice and equality for all to become a reality.

3 The vineyard of the kingdom of heaven
Read Matthew 20:1–34

The parable we encounter in this passage is unique to Matthew's Gospel. As such, it may be considered an insight into the special focus of the Gospel, and reflect something of the writer's understanding of life around him in first-century Palestine.

This story of the vineyard workers may well be taken straight from agricultural life in a Palestinian village. Like many of Jesus' parables, it draws on images and practices familiar to the crowds who gathered around Jesus to listen to him. Such familiarity would have caught the crowd's attention and helped them understand the religious teaching Jesus wanted to convey.

Like many of Jesus' parables, though, the story has an unexpected twist. Even in first-century Palestine, the concept of equal work for equal pay was an established principle. But here we find the vineyard owner paying the same wage to the labourers, regardless of how much or how little time they worked during the day. Such an uneconomical practice must have taken the crowd by surprise. What lord or owner would make such a foolishly generous offer?

The clue is in the last verse of the story, in a saying that Jesus has used a number of times, and one that was no doubt familiar to his disciples and regular followers: 'the last shall be first and the first shall be last'. With this phrase, the vineyard is revealed as the kingdom of heaven, and the owner is, of course, God—the God who is as generous to those who seek his kingdom at the last minute as he is to those who found it much earlier.

This may have been difficult for the disciples to hear, especially James and John! After all, their mother's request makes it clear that they and the other disciples had given up everything they had to follow Jesus, with the expectation of heavenly reward. Now those who would join the movement later, who have not given up so much or suffered as long, would be greeted by God as equals.

Matthew may have included this story to defend Jesus' inclusion of sinners in the kingdom as well as the righteous. Or he may have meant it as explanation for why Gentiles (the last) should be part of God's kingdom as much as the Jews (the first). Whatever his reason, the parable reminds us of God's overwhelming grace, a grace that is inclusive of all who would seek God.

4   Palm Sunday   *Read Matthew 21:1–11*

Jesus has finally arrived in Jerusalem, the city of the great king (5:35). He is greeted by the adoring crowds, who sing 'Hosanna', and hail him as Son of David. Despite this royal title, Jesus enters the city in humble fashion, mounted on a donkey. This entry into Jerusalem marks the beginning of a new section in the Gospel. Jesus' ministry in the countryside has come to an end, and the fulfilment of his predicted fate is at hand.

What must have been going through the mind of Jesus and the disciples as he entered the city to this tumultuous praise? The disciples may well have found a new hope in this reception of

Jesus—surely such a loved and popular figure could not be hastening towards his own death. The thoughts of Jesus may well have centred on the irony of the situation. He is hailed as Son of David, the Messiah of Israel, which indeed he is. Yet he is probably aware that many of these same people will shortly reject him as such, and contribute to his demise on the cross.

No doubt popular expectation was for a Messiah who would free Israel from the grasp of the hated Romans. When Jesus shows he is in fact a humble Messiah, obedient even to the point of dying an ignoble death, popular opinion turns against him. The crowds no doubt failed to understand the concept of a kingdom that was not a national-political identity, but rather one that transcended earthly bounds and was universal in its scope.

In many ways, we in the 21st century live a life dedicated to tangible success in much the same way this ancient crowd did. We tend to give more credit, and more plausibility, to those who show the external trappings of success. If such a person fails to live up to the promise we saw in them, then they are rejected as no longer having much to offer us. So it is worth holding the story of Palm Sunday before us, to help keep our perspective focused on what is really important.

5   Visiting the temple   *Read Matthew 21:12–22*

After his triumphal entry into Jerusalem, Jesus continues to keep himself firmly in the public eye. His next act is to visit the centre of the Jewish faith, the temple. But he has not come to worship or to offer sacrifice in the temple. He does not submit himself or his disciples to the authority of the priests. Rather, he performs a symbolic act of purification in his clearing out of all the traders and money changers, crying out words of scriptural prophecy as he overturns the tables.

Jesus is clearly challenging the established ritual of the temple, and the accepted way of making one's self right with God. He has made it clear that the kingdom of God, as expressed by his presence, is not about sacrifice and silver. Rather, it is about mercy and wholeness, and he demonstrates this by healing the blind and the lame.

The singing of the children interprets the events to those who watch or hear the story. With the extraordinary perception of those who see clearly, the children proclaim Jesus as Son of David. They recognize that the kingdom of God has entered the human realm, and the old order is reversed. The last (the unclean, the deformed and the imperfect) are now first. The ritually clean and their support groups are now placed last.

Of course, such actions do not go unchallenged by the religious authorities. Matthew depicts the chief priests and the scribes as objecting to mercy, to healing, and to the praise of children. They fail to see that 'something greater than the temple is here' (12:6). They do not see that it is Jesus, rather than the temple, who offers real communion between God and humanity.

The cursing of the fig tree follows on from the incident at the temple. It links the closing incidents of the previous day with the new day about to unfold. Like the temple, the fig tree is beautiful to look at, with its covering of green leaves. Like the temple also, the fig tree bears no fruit. The lack of fruit is a scriptural motif that is quite disturbing. In Matthew's Gospel, particularly, it denotes a lack of faith, a lack of comprehension and an inability to offer or receive the gifts of the kingdom. The withering of the fig tree is a clear demonstration of the fate of those who do not believe, and who bear no fruit. It may also foreshadow the destruction of the Jerusalem temple.

6   Parables of the kingdom   *Read Matthew 21:23–45*

This section has often been seen as rather difficult to interpret and understand. At first glance, Jesus' debate with the religious authorities and the story of the two sons do not seem to have much in common.

At first we have Jesus displaying his skills as a teacher and debater. By clever questioning, Jesus manages to back the priests and elders into a corner. Fearful of hazarding an opinion, they are forced to answer that they do not know. Unable to formulate an opinion regarding John the Baptist, they are also incapable of judging Jesus.

This exchange with the religious leaders introduces a series of conflicts that will continue through the next few chapters. It demonstrates how Jesus' authority undercuts all sources of human power. It also demonstrates the blindness and disobedience of those who would claim such authority for themselves.

This is the purpose of the story of the two sons. Each son represents the two responses to Jesus' message: those who accept it and those who reject it. But there is a twist—neither character (and the group that each character represents) is immediately obvious in their intentions. The first son refuses to obey the command of his father. He later repents of this, and goes to do the work his father asked him to. The second son agrees to go and do the work, but fails to keep his promise.

Matthew makes it clear in his Gospel that it is the outcasts of the current system (prostitutes, tax collectors) who end up doing the will of the Father, despite their lowly status. They have heard the message of John the Baptist and Jesus and believed it. In contrast, it is the respectable religious leaders who claim obedience to the Father, but in fact do not follow his wishes. They rejected the teachings of John the Baptist and now reject Jesus, despite the obvious signs of the kingdom that accompany his ministry.

The second parable strengthens the message. The leaders—represented by the tenants—are shown to be not only disobedient, but murderers as well. Their failure to hear and understand culminates in the removal of the one who is truly the messenger of the father. Instead of assuring their inheritance of the kingdom by this action, they in fact will be rejected.

The kingdom is open to whoever repents and trusts in God. Status, tradition and piety are by themselves meaningless. Only by genuine attempts to discern and follow the will of God can one inherit the kingdom of God.

GUIDELINES

Loving God, Creator and redeemer of us all,
We praise you for your greatness:
your wisdom and creativity are seen
in heaven and earth which you have made.

We praise you for your saving acts:
your grace and truth are revealed to us
in Jesus whom you sent as Saviour.
We praise you for your presence with us:
your gifts and power are given to us through the Holy Spirit.

Claim our life and work for your holy purpose.
Help us to serve the people in your world
who are in need of your love and mercy,
remembering the promise which Jesus gave
of your mercy and justice and comfort.

We are your people, and you are our God.
Put your will into our minds, and write it into our hearts.
Put your song into our spirits, that we may proclaim with joy,
'Blessed is he who comes in the name of the Lord!'
Therefore we will glorify your name,
through Jesus Christ our Lord.
Amen.

---

26 MARCH–1 APRIL   MATTHEW 22:1—25:46

1   The messianic invitation   *Read Matthew 22:1–14*

Again we find Jesus using a parable about a familiar event, a wedding, to explain to the crowd something about the kingdom of heaven. Once more he highlights the Jewish leadership's lack of response to God's invitation to join with him in the kingdom. He also shows that it is the outcasts and sinners on the fringe of society who will receive this unexpected invitation from God to join him at the heavenly banquet.

The call to come to the wedding banquet initially goes out to the expected invitees, to tell them the time of the banquet is at hand and they should make haste and come. Unfortunately, many of the invited guests do not take the call seriously and go on with their regular business. A few, like the workers in the vineyard, actually mistreat and kill the messengers.

This parable moves to the next stage of revelation about the kingdom. The first invited guests represent the Jewish leadership, who reject Jesus' invitation and persecute his followers. Their rejection allows the invitation to be broadened to include all people, both good and bad. However, the final verses indicate that righteousness (the wedding garment) is still an issue—it is no use answering the invitation if one still follows the ways of the unrighteous.

The parable contains a grim warning to those who considered themselves sure of the messianic invitation. Those who are the chosen ones are not in fact among the elect, but are only called. Their tradition does not guarantee them inclusion. In fact, their refusal and subsequent mistreatment of God's servants can only end in the ultimate destruction of them and their city. Those who do respond to the invitation must nevertheless respond appropriately. It is not sufficient to have said 'yes' to Jesus (see 7:21–23); one must also show the fruit of the kingdom, wearing righteousness and obedience to the Father as symbolized by the wedding robe.

Like Matthew's ill-clad wedding guest, it is very easy to identify oneself with the righteous, by entering the Church, joining in the Christian community and espousing a life of faith. In his Gospel, Matthew recognizes that such actions are not necessarily indicative of true faith. The same is true today. Only by consciously living out our faith, through our words and our deeds, can we truly hope to be numbered among those at the banquet table.

2 The first commandment   *Read Matthew 22:23–46*

In this section we find Jesus again debating with some of the Jewish leaders. Both Pharisees and Sadducees seem to have decided to test Jesus in debate on some of the finer points of the law. First the Pharisees ask him about tax (this section was discussed with 17:24–27). Then the Sadducees decide to quiz Jesus about resurrection and the so-called 'Levirate law' of marriage.

The Sadducees were a conservative, affluent group who may have been among the priests who looked after the temple. They considered the first five books of the Hebrew Bible to be the true word of God. They upheld the Levirate law found in the code of Moses, which allowed a brother to marry his deceased brother's wife in order to produce an heir for the deceased person. They did not believe in resurrection, which was a much later idea.

These two beliefs lie behind their question to Jesus, which could not have been sincere, since they did not hold any belief in resurrection. They probably thought their example of the woman and the seven brothers showed resurrection to be an absurd concept, and expected it to embarrass or disconcert Jesus in any answer he might give. Instead, Jesus asserts that the Sadducees are wrong in their scriptural understanding—they have set limits on a God whose power has no limits. He also points out that their concept of resurrection is based on the fallacy that it will be an extension of life as it was on earth.

Jesus maintains that life in the resurrection will be completely transformed. As evidence, he offers Exodus 3:16, a verse chosen from the Sadducees' limited canon. God does not say that once he was the God of Abraham, Isaac and Jacob. He says he still is their God, implying that these ancients were still living somehow in his presence.

The crowds are astonished, but not the Pharisees. They prepare another assault on Jesus' integrity by asking him to describe the greatest law. Jesus' answer is simple: love God with all your heart, and such love will be reflected in love for your neighbour. This double command, to love God and neighbour, is truly a vital command for all to follow. It at once gives to God the reverence and obedience that God is due, and it allows us to treat others as we would have God deal with us—with forgiveness, mercy and grace.

3   Woe to you!   *Read Matthew 23:1–39*

This chapter is one of the passages that is difficult for us to understand accurately. When taken at a literal level, it has led to modern interpretations that are as damaging as they are unfair. The assumption is that the Pharisees and scribes are the 'bad guys', and this has led to the belief that 'Pharisee' equals 'hypocrite'. It is disturbing that such a stereotype has found its way into the language of our modern Church. Equally disturbing is the notion that Jesus here seems to contradict his own dictums about loving one's enemy and turning the other cheek. So what is really happening here?

It is clear that Jesus respects the *position* of the scribes and Pharisees. His particular problem with them stems from their love of show and desire to impress others with their public piety. Part of the explanation lies with the accepted prophetic rhetoric of the time. The extended polemic against the scribes and the Pharisees in Matthew 23 echoes the hostility shown by most of the prophets to the Jewish leadership of their times. Like the prophets, this intensity of feeling was in part due to the need of Matthew to convince his readers and listeners that it was Jesus who had the true authority from God. The expression of woes in this form can also be found in prophetic scripture, as an expression of divine judgment (Isaiah 5:8,18f.; Habakkuk 2:6–17) and divine pity.

Another part of the explanation lies with exactly whom Matthew is addressing. Jesus has made it quite clear in earlier passages that it is the humble who will be exalted. Here we see what happens in a religious community where the arrogant feel that they are indeed the first and best in that community. Matthew is warning his readers, the members of the Christian community, not to adopt the behaviour and attitudes shown by some other religious leaders.

Jesus does not leave the people he criticizes without hope, however. The last verse suggests that they can still turn to righteousness and greet Jesus as the one 'who comes in the name of the Lord', and still be welcome in the new kingdom.

The warning is still pertinent for us. Leaders of the Christian community today must resist the temptation to capitalize on perceived power and status. Following Jesus means leading a life characterized by service and humility, not by titles or distinctions.

4 The end of time *Read Matthew 24:1–31*

The signs listed by Jesus as taking place during the end of the world are catastrophic. They include wars, famines and earthquakes, persecution, betrayal and death, lawlessness and the appearance of false prophets and messiahs. Even in the heavens the signs are ominous—the stars will fall and the sun and moon will disappear. The events listed form a picture of universal and cataclysmic suffering; these are signs that announce the nearness of the day of judgment by God, and the beginning of a new age in which the righteous will be rewarded and the wicked punished. At the end of this terrible period of suffering, Jesus will return as the triumphant Son of man to judge Israel and the nations of the world.

What a grim picture the words of Jesus paint! Yet many of these catastrophic events have become all too common in the history of the human race. Nearly every generation of humanity has had to deal with war, famine, natural disasters and prophecies of doom, and also with the fear and anxiety that they inspire. There have been very few periods of time when peace and prosperity were the dominant features of the world.

Yet Jesus can still offer a word of hope to the disciples, a hope that remains current for us today. To the disciples, Jesus states that these disasters will pass away, that they are but signs of his imminent return and the establishment of the power of God. But the most powerful gift of hope that Jesus gives is the promise that his words will not pass away—the words of hope, of mercy, of acceptance of sinners, and of the power and love of God.

It is this assurance—that God is with us and loves us—that has enabled many generations of faithful believers to keep going in the face of persecution, trouble and grief. It is this assurance which has enabled believers to reach out to others in our turbulent world and show them the compassion of Jesus and the love of God through help in the form of food, water, shelter, clothing and care. It is this assurance that is the foundation of our faith.

5   Watch and wait   *Read Matthew 24:32—25:30*

Have you ever sat at home during the day, waiting for a tradesman to stop by as promised to repair a faulty service or appliance? And after you have waited for two to three hours past the time allotted for the repair, you finally decide to leave—and you just miss the tradesman by a few minutes! Most of us have probably found ourselves in such a situation a number of times. In our busy society of tight schedules, even a short delay or unexpected wait can throw out our timetable and cause us to become impatient so that we feel there is no point in waiting any longer.

In today's passage, Jesus shows that this unwillingness to wait was also a common occurrence in first-century Palestine. In the parables he tells, however, giving up waiting because of the lateness of an expected caller takes on a sinister dimension. Jesus has already spoken to the disciples about his death, resurrection and triumphant return. In relation to this return, he now stresses that there will not be any special signs to warn anyone when his coming will be. To complicate matters further, it will be at a time when everybody is going about their normal business just as they would do on a normal day. Those who are impatient and decide he is not coming may well be caught unawares and miss the opportunity to enter the kingdom of heaven.

The underlying meaning of most of these parables is clear. Our daily existence should not be about self-interested or violent activities, but about accepting our responsibilities, however humble, and carrying them out faithfully. By doing this, we remain obedient to God. The last of the parables is a little different though. Building on the previous stories of being prepared, it goes further and suggests that not only should we do our tasks as faithful followers of Jesus, but we should also try to use our gifts to contribute even more to the kingdom of God. In this story, to have gifts for the kingdom and fail to use them is almost as bad as being unrighteous. This parable was, and still is, aimed at the leaders in the Church. Those who have gifts should use them to the benefit of all, as such service in God's name is of incalculable value to the community.

6 Sheep and goats *Read Matthew 25:31–46*

This particular description of the judgment is, by New Testament standards, rather unusual. In fact, it is unique to the Gospel of Matthew. It is unique in its use of sheep and goats as symbols for the righteous and unrighteous. It is unique in its definition of who the righteous are. In fact, it is unique in the New Testament. It is unique because in this particular parable, Jesus makes an astounding pronouncement—that when people perform good deeds for some of their poorer fellow human beings, they, in fact, are ministering to Jesus himself. Both sheep and goats are judged on the basis of their actions. They either helped those in need, or they did not.

This parable is troubling. Its message does not always sit easily with those who profess Christianity today. Why is this? Because Jesus the judge does not separate the righteous people on the basis of their faith, or because they chose to follow him, or even because they belonged to one of the Christian communities. The staggering message that this parable proclaims is that neither belief in Jesus, nor knowingly following his teachings, forms part of the pre-requisites for entry into the kingdom of heaven. Indeed, these righteous 'sheep' that are rewarded by the gift of eternal life are ignorant of any idea that Jesus was involved in their actions. Perhaps they are the kind of people that Paul talks about in Romans 2, who are obedient to God's command instinctively, without realizing who God or Jesus are.

Jesus identifies deliberately with the powerless, the weak, the despised and the tortured. He identifies with the world's outcasts and asks us to minister to them in our faith. He teaches us the lesson that love for neighbour cannot be separated from love for the Lord. He stresses that faith must manifest itself in deeds of charity.

We can discover the body of Christ in a lonely neighbour, a refugee, a troubled teenager, a single parent or a lonely person, or someone dying and in need of comfort. Wherever we are tempted to draw back or turn away from someone in need, or to avoid someone's pain, then we turn from Jesus. As Jesus did, we can learn to identify with the pain of others, and to share with others our compassion and our wealth, material and immaterial. It is then we truly show the face of God to all.

GUIDELINES

A story is told of St Francis of Assisi, the monk who became famous for his piety, compassion and poverty. One day he said to a young novitiate monk, 'Let us go down to the town and preach to the people.' So the pair of them set off, down the hill to the town. Once they arrived there, St Francis led the way through the streets and alleyways. They stopped to speak to beggars, and greeted old and infirm women. They spoke to the children playing in the street, and soothed those who had sorrows or grief. They shared their lunch with a crippled man, and offered prayers of comfort to parents who had lost a child. At the end of the day, the two returned to the monastery at the top of the hill. 'St Francis', said the puzzled young monk, 'I thought we were going to preach in the town?' St Francis replied, 'The people saw our care for them, and observed our courteous manner. They knew where we came from and the God we represented. Yes, we preached.'

Lord make me an instrument of your peace;
where there is hatred let me sow love;
where there is injury, pardon;
where there is discord, union;
where there is doubt, faith;
where there is despair, hope;
where there is darkness, light;
where there is sadness, joy;
for your mercy and truth's sake.

O Divine Master,
grant that I may not so much seek
to be consoled as to console,
to be understood as to understand,
to be loved as to love.
For it is in giving that we receive;
it is in pardoning that we are pardoned;
it is in dying that we are born to eternal life. Amen.

2–8 APRIL   **MATTHEW 26:1–75**

---

1   **The betrayal of Jesus**   *Read Matthew 26:1–5, 14–16, 47–56*

The story of Jesus' betrayal, arrest, trials and crucifixion is well known in the Christian tradition. In reading through Matthew's account of these events, we will note its distinctive features.

The passages chosen for today have a unifying theme running through them—that of betrayal. At what was to be the last gathering of all the disciples for a meal, protestations of unflinching loyalty and devotion to Jesus are numerous. After announcing that he will be betrayed by one who is eating with him, Jesus is questioned by all the disciples as to which one of them is the betrayer. Despite his clandestine meeting with the chief priests, even Judas adds his declaration of innocence to that of the other disciples. For those who can read the original text in Greek, Matthew has inserted here a double irony, for Judas' question in Greek explicitly expects the answer 'No!' The other disciple Matthew focuses on at this gathering is, of course, Peter, whose protestations of loyalty are perhaps the loudest of all. Peter announces he will die rather than betray Jesus. The other disciples reinforce this, all claiming death would be preferable to betrayal.

One of the most disturbing features of this simple meal together must surely be the disciples' need to ask Jesus who the betrayer would be. His question seems to prompt a lot of soul-searching among them, requiring them to look deep into themselves and their motivations. The response to the results of this soul-searching is obviously disconcerting to the disciples, who cover their discomfort with questions and assertions of remaining steadfast. The response and subsequent actions of the disciples show that there is very little distance between assurances of loyalty and actions of desertion. Perhaps this is why Jesus had continually stressed the need for actions to demonstrate faith.

If the disciples, with their intimate knowledge of Jesus and their close relationship to him needed to ask such questions concerning their loyalty, how much more should we, who did not have the privilege of personally being with Jesus, ask this question of ourselves? Though Jesus no doubt still grieves at our own weakness, he still offers the hope that we can share a future with him. God forgives human frailty, understands the limitations of humanity. Like the disciples, with faith we can again rally to follow the will of God.

2 The anointing of Jesus *Read Matthew 26:6–13*

The story of Jesus' anointing by a woman is a familiar one. Most of us have heard it many times, and are not surprised or shocked by it. However, when this story was first told, many of those who read or heard the story would have been very shocked.

Try to imagine someone like the Pope, or the Archbishop of Canterbury, going about their business with women of dubious reputation appearing to offer to massage them with oil. Most people would be horrified! A woman gatecrashing a private male party was an event which the ancient world would have decried, a scene which would evoke disgust, and a sense of uncleanness. After all, women were not allowed any say in leadership, or religion. They could not own land. They did not eat with their men at important meetings. They did not learn to read and write. They were considered very inferior. Now one of these women has entered the house as an uninvited guest at a dinner party. She is determined enough to run the risk of being thrown out by Simon and the disciples. She is probably a 'sinner', earning money by dubious means, but she does not come empty-handed. In fact, her actions show that her understanding is greater than the disciples.

The woman anoints Jesus with the ointment she has brought with her. Anointing someone with fragrant oil was a great tribute to them, a recognition of their importance. The disciples were angry—here was not only a gatecrashing woman but also a flagrant waste of money. The woman has come to perform this rite for Jesus. She is unwelcome to all but him. Jesus understands that love undergirds her actions—love for Jesus, and love for God. His response to her is one of affirmation. God belongs in the midst of the marginalized and outcast. Jesus, because he is from God, can do no more than the will of God, which is to meet outcasts and sinners with compassion and blessing.

For us, the blessing in this story is the model that Jesus offers to the Church. He offers acceptance and hope both to the sinners and the righteous of this world. By following Jesus' example, we can build communities of safety, acceptance, forgiveness and love. By doing so, we unlock the gateway for many others to enter into the kingdom of God.

3 The Passover meal *Read Matthew 26:17–30*

Jesus and his disciples were celebrating a time-honoured Jewish tradition when they sat down to eat together for the last time—the festival of Passover. This festival commemorated an important event in Jewish history, around the time of Israel's exodus from Egypt. It reminded Jews that the angel of death had 'passed over' the homes of the Israelites in Egypt, just as their ancestors had 'passed over' the Red Sea into freedom. For Christians, this last Passover meal was the beginning of one of the most fundamental Christian sacraments, the sacrament of the eucharist, or communion. During the meal, Jesus takes bread and wine and offers it to the disciples. He asks them to remember him and the sacrifice that he was about to make for all humankind. He leaves this communion meal as his parting gift.

Sharing any sort of meal with a group of intimate friends is a declaration of trust and friendship. For early Christians, remembering this last meal of Jesus became an act of worship, a time of spiritual significance and sharing in the ministry and person of Jesus. This commemorative act quickly became known as the Eucharist, a service of thanksgiving for the life, death and resurrection of Jesus. The Christian covenant, like that of the older Jewish covenant, was a pact made in blood, and therefore marked by sacrifice. Jesus' words, 'This cup is the new covenant made in my blood', made it clear that it is the blood of Christ which seals the new covenant between God and human beings.

When we gather together as Christians to celebrate this meal, past, present and future come together to remind us of God's grace and mercy. We look back to the past with gratitude to the redemptive death of Jesus on the cross. We celebrate the present, in a symbolic act that reminds us afresh of the grace of God and how that grace has given us the gift of salvation. We also look forward to the future that Jesus promised, a future where the kingdom of God will unite all the faithful together in a world cleansed of sin and evil.

4 The Mount of Olives *Read Matthew 26:31–46*

To the uninitiated, the story of Jesus in the garden of Gethsemane presents a picture of loneliness, despair and personal agony, a picture of hopelessness and abandonment. For Christians, this night is commemorated by a solemn vigil in churches throughout the world. On the night of Maundy Thursday, we remember the betrayal, arrest, mocking, scourging and death of Jesus. It is designed to evoke in us a reflective response, which transports us to keep watch with Jesus in the Garden of Gethsemane, and enter into the pain of his prayers and reflections.

It is the last time that Jesus will be together with the disciples. Matthew again highlights the disciples' inability to rise to the occasion and comfort Jesus in his last hours of freedom. Only the most trusted accompany Jesus into the gloom of the garden so he can pray to help alleviate his sorrow and anxiety. In this moving scene, Jesus pours out his soul to his Father in heaven. The agony he experiences is real; his cry to be spared the suffering is the cry of someone who does not think he can go on.

Christians through the ages have wondered why the Son of God felt such agony, why this period of self-doubt and anguish occurred at all. They forget that Jesus was in his life just like the people he ministered to. Foregoing any special status or privilege his unique role may have brought him, Jesus experienced joy, pain and sadness like those around him. Like many of the poor or outcast, Jesus stated that he had no place to lay his head. Like many who were condemned for their beliefs, he experienced hatred and physical abuse at the hands of his accusers.

Jesus knew what it was to be human. We have seen that the Son of God stood deliberately and voluntarily in the shoes of the powerless, the weak, the defenceless, the despised and the tortured. Though he prayed and agonized over his fate, his obedience to God never faltered. Now, Jesus prepares himself to offer the ultimate sacrifice—his life.

5 The temple trial *Read Matthew 26:57–68*

The trial of Jesus raises in a most acute form one of the central issues that has run throughout Matthew's story of the life of Jesus. The question, 'Who killed Jesus?', has most often been answered, simply, 'The Jews killed Jesus.' Today's passage recounts the role played by the high priest and the Sanhedrin (the council of priests and scribes) in bringing Jesus to his death.

Jesus remains silent when false witnesses accuse him of claiming to destroy the temple. He ignores the high priest's accusation that he has messianic pretensions. Instead, he speaks in a way that identifies himself with the coming Son of man. The blasphemous nature of this claim does not escape the high priest; and so the plot which was hatched at 26:3–4 can come to fruition. Jesus deserves death, and so the Roman authorities will be pressured to execute him (27:1–2).

Historical evidence from other sources suggests that the account which Matthew (and the other evangelists) have told may not be accurate. The death sentence was not supposed to be given on the same day that the trial began—an overnight 'cooling off period' was needed before condemning a criminal to death. Nor was the Sanhedrin supposed to meet at night, as this account indicates (see 27:1). These difficulties tend to suggest that the early Christian depiction of the Jewish authorities may have been motivated by a desire to denigrate them.

Elsewhere in Matthew's Gospel, this tendency is evident: in Jesus' slanderous attack on the Pharisees and scribes (chapter 23), in the way the Jewish authorities bulldoze Pilate into accepting their wish (27:15ff), and in the infamous cry of the Jewish people when Jesus is sent to be crucified (27:25). As he writes his Gospel, Matthew takes many opportunities to show how evil had permeated the Jewish authorities. He also firmly excuses Pilate from his responsibilities in sentencing Jesus to death (27:24).

At many points in Christian history, the Jews as a whole have been depicted in similar fashion. The accusation that 'the Jews killed Jesus'—hardened into the strident charge, 'the Jews killed God'—has done immense damage. Crusades, pogroms and ultimately the horrors of the Holocaust have been the result of this callous view of the Jews. However, the denigration of Jewish leaders in Matthew's account relates to a specific historical circumstance. When today we read these early accounts of the death of Jesus, we cannot afford to perpetuate a stereotype that is unfair and inaccurate. Using the passion narrative as a justification for anti-Semitic attitudes and actions can no longer be tolerated.

6 Peter's denial   *Read Matthew 26:31–35, 69–75*

The story of Peter's denial is a dramatic interruption in the narrative of Jesus' trials and sufferings. Peter's cowardly behaviour is deliberately contrasted with Jesus' truthful confession and courage.

How wretched the unfortunate Peter must have felt when confronted by his own frailty! Only hours before he had been steadfast in his vows of loyalty and willingness to die for his beloved master. When faced with persecution and possible death, the desire to avoid trouble and save himself overcame any feelings of loyalty to Jesus that Peter may have felt. Now, his only companions are his bitterness of soul and weakness of spirit. In a small space of time, Peter has forgotten that he was designated 'rock' by Jesus, and reverted to his former stance of decrying Jesus' suffering as Messiah.

There is a warning here to all would-be followers of Jesus. That Peter, the designated foundation of the Church, could exhibit such human frailty is a lesson to all those who are over-confident in their faith. Matthew was obviously aware that human weakness, especially in times of turmoil, would always be an issue that needed to be confronted and addressed, for even the most dedicated of disciples would experience doubt and fear. Despite this acknowledgment of the frailty of the human condition, there is nevertheless hope for the disciples and the fledgling followers of Jesus who struggle with their faith and their mission. When faith breaks down, and human weakness comes to the fore, the forgiveness and mercy of God will also be present, offering hope and restoration.

Unlike the writer of the Gospel of Mark, where the disciples are regularly seen as having no faith, Matthew teaches that even a very small amount of faith, coupled with the grace of God, will be enough in the end to overcome persecution, fear, and even death itself. At the end of the Gospel, Peter is summoned by the risen Jesus along with the other disciples, and entrusted with the task of making disciples of all the nations. Tradition informs us that eventually Peter did lose his life for his faith, and faced death with courage and strength.

Peter's story offers hope to us all. No matter how we might stumble in our faith journey, the love of God will be there to strengthen and guide us. Therefore, we too can become God's emissaries among our communities.

GUIDELINES

Our faith as followers of Jesus calls us into discipleship, and like Jesus, it could lead us into difficult, dangerous situations. When we choose to follow Jesus, our lives, like his, are pointed in a certain direction. When we choose to travel the road to Jerusalem with Jesus, we are called to walk with other human beings on life's journey, and to minister to them in various ways. This means helping others where we can, setting time aside for sharing the joys and sorrows of others' lives, and taking action on matters that affect people.

It is very easy for fallible people to become afraid, like Peter. Our concerns about ourselves can harden us, causing us to play down our faith and concentrate on our own lives. We fail to acknowledge Jesus; we fail to recognize the needs of others; we fail to be the people that God wants us to be.

One of the central strands of our faith is our belief that God shows us grace, compassion and love. Such gifts strengthen our faith to enable us to transcend threatening situations. Should we stumble on our journey, or experience deep doubts or fear, God the compassionate one enables us to keep going. As the Church, we are called to bear witness to that grace, not just in the words we say, but in the very essence of our lifestyle and way of living. Thus we can help others as they struggle and journey along their road of faith.

It is this witness to Christ that sustains and supports the work of the gospel in every congregation. It is our faith and trust in God, and his love and grace towards us, that keeps us moving along the road of discipleship, as we offer service, support and prayer for each other and for the community. May we continue to find hope and strength in our faith journeys. May we continue to give thanks for God's gracious presence with us.

1   Trial by Pilate   *Read Matthew 27:1–26*

The Jewish authorities wish Jesus to die. Because the Romans rule the region, it is they who must execute Jesus. So, the Jewish authorities force the hand of Pilate, the Roman governor; then they persuade the crowd to back them. For Matthew, the antagonism of these authorities towards Jesus is unrelieved. They represent the synagogue leaders of Matthew's own day, from whom his own community has become firmly alienated.

As events follow their relentless course towards the death of Jesus, the narrative offers glimpses of a number of figures who are swept up, somewhat unwillingly, in what takes place. Judas is hit by the realization of where his betrayal of Jesus will lead. In remorse, he repents and returns his blood money to the authorities. The authorities are callous in their reply, 'What is that to us?' Left with the money they had paid Judas, they simply rationalize their subsequent action.

Pilate's wife attempts to intervene on behalf of Jesus. A Gentile woman, she reminds us of other surprising believers in Jesus, both Gentiles (8:5–13) and women (15:21–28). She is the first to dream in this Gospel since Joseph and the wise men. Like their dreams, hers contains a clear message from God: Jesus is innocent. Nevertheless, Pilate resists her pleas; he is, by now, thoroughly cowed by the demands of the crowd. He washes his hands, attempting to purge his guilt. Ironically, however, he cannot escape from the consequences of his actions. He is remembered in history as the weak pawn of the Jewish authorities. Other historical sources indicate that Pilate was a fierce and unrelenting ruler who was not afraid to inflict harsh penalties on the Jews. It is likely that Matthew is lessening the blame that might have been placed on Pilate for the death of Jesus.

The Jewish crowd is made to take the responsibility for the death of Jesus. Their cry reflects the traditional Jewish idea that guilt is inherited and passed on down the generations. In one fell swoop, Matthew attempts to turn the responsibility from the Romans to the Jews as a whole. As we noted last week, the wider context shows that it is Matthew's own polemic that is at work in his account.

Only Jesus remains in full control of his actions. He refuses to plead his own case when brought before the Jewish authorities. He remains resolutely silent, for the die is cast: 'he *must* undergo great suffering... and be killed' (16:21), for 'the Son of man came... to give his life as a ransom for many' (20:28).

2 The road to the cross *Read Matthew 27:27–44*

Jesus is sentenced to death. The charge reveals the Roman perception of Jesus as 'King of the Jews', an accusation of fomenting a political rebellion against the Roman rulers. Jesus shares his fate with others who are (perhaps correctly) accused of revolutionary insurrection. Although innocent in Matthew's eyes, Jesus will not avoid death on the cross—the typical Roman punishment for political criminals. The crucifixion of Jesus reminds us of the way he lived his life. He kept company with those on the margins of society—the disabled, the unclean, the mentally ill, women, people of ill repute such as tax collectors and prostitutes. In his death, he is in the company of political rebels.

Matthew's account of Jesus' crucifixion has many resonances with Hebrew scriptures. Jesus goes to his death an innocent man, righteous before God. To a Jew such as Matthew, the psalms of the righteous sufferer provide a rich resource for describing the significance of what Jesus endures. Psalm 22 especially expresses the despair of the righteous sufferer, who believes that God has abandoned him (Psalm 22:1; quoted by Jesus at 27:46).

Jesus is mocked by the Roman soldiers, those passing by, the Jewish authorities and the criminals being crucified with him. Such mocking reflects the fate of the righteous person (Psalm 22:7–8). The words of the authorities, 'Let God deliver him', repeat the cry of those who mock the righteous person (Psalm 22:8). When the soldiers strip Jesus, divide his clothes and cast lots for them, they are enacting the evil of those who mock the righteous person (Psalm 22:18). When they offer Jesus wine mixed with vinegar, they implement the actions noted in another psalm of the righteous sufferer (Psalm 69:21).

The allusions to the psalms hint at the ultimate vindication that God will give to the person who suffers unjustly. Such psalms always ended with shouts of praise to God for eventually helping. Yet the story of Jesus seems not to follow this pathway, at least in the events which follow immediately. Jesus is destined to die; although he is depicted as a righteous sufferer, it appears to the scornful people who surround him that God has failed to intervene to save him.

3   The death of Jesus   *Read Matthew 27:45–56*

The scene of Jesus' death forms a sombre climax to the passion narrative. Jesus expresses his desolation in the words of the psalmist (Psalm 22:1). In Mark's account, the centurion makes his confession that Jesus is the Son of God immediately after he sees Jesus die (Mark 15:39). In Matthew's account, it is not only the centurion, but also all his troops who are guarding Jesus, who make this confession. The confession does not come immediately after Jesus dies; rather, it follows a sequence of extraordinary events: the tearing of the temple veil, an earthquake, the opening of the tombs and the raising of the saints. These events are reported only in Matthew's Gospel; they are signs that the end is near (compare 24:29–31). They provide God's response to the death of Jesus; for Matthew, this death will usher in the kingdom.

The confession by centurion and the guard, 'Truly this man was the Son of God', parallels that of the disciples in 14:33. It answers a question that has been earlier raised by the people and leaders in 27:40–44: Is Jesus the Son of God as he claimed? Both confessions that Jesus is Son of God are elicited as a result of supernatural happenings. It is when God acts that the true identity of Jesus can be perceived.

We saw earlier (8:5–13) how the faith of a Gentile centurion was held up to the Jewish leadership who had rejected Jesus as a model for those wishing to inherit the kingdom. Here a Gentile centurion and his guard stand as models of those who recognize the divine appointment of Jesus, and are prepared to acknowledge it. They are faithful, in contrast to the Jewish leaders, who not only fail to recognise who Jesus is during his ministry, but also fail to appreciate the divine confirmation provided by God after Jesus dies. Their confession fulfils Psalm 22:27–31; God's deliverance is attested by the (Gentile) nations.

To this is added the testimony of the women who had been disciples of Jesus during his time in Galilee (vv. 55–56). Their faithful presence contrasts with the desertion, denial and betrayal of Jesus by his male disciples. At the critical moment of Jesus' death, faithfulness is shown by unexpected groups: Gentiles and women.

4 Burial and resurrection   *Read Matthew 27:57–61; 28:1–10*

The women will carry through their fidelity to Jesus in the following scenes, when they attend the burial of Jesus and then return after the Sabbath to anoint his body. In this, they are carrying out the required customs of their culture. They are joined by a benefactor, Joseph of Arimathea, who makes his own tomb available as the resting place for the body of Jesus.

There are some surprises in these verses. The normal Roman practice was for the bodies of criminals to be thrown into a common pit outside the city; although often crucified victims would be left hanging for some days after death. The reverent disposal of Jesus' body signals that he is different. This will be confirmed by the stories of his resurrection appearances that follow.

The account of the empty tomb (vv. 1–10) bears a striking resemblance to the distinctive Matthean account of the death of Jesus (27:50–56). Each scene includes an earthquake, the opening of tombs, and the resurrection of the dead. In each case, also, there are Roman guards and women disciples who are present as witnesses. The fear that the guards exhibit when they encounter the angel repeats the fear that they experienced when the resurrected saints walked through the holy city after Jesus had died. The women will experience the same fear when the risen Jesus appears to them as they are leaving the tomb.

Such a doubling-up of 'special effects' has a dramatic impact. As Matthew draws near to the end of his Gospel, he emphasizes yet again the central role that Jesus plays in God's scheme of things. The earthquake and the raising of the dead point again to the new kingdom which is to be inaugurated. The fact that these signs are noted both when Jesus dies and when his tomb is found empty underline that Jesus is the one who inaugurates the coming of this new kingdom.

In Matthew's Gospel (as also in Luke and John), the risen Jesus appears first to his women followers (not so, however, according to Paul: see 1 Corinthians 15:3–8). In this scene, the risen Jesus commissions these women to be the first evangelists, when he commands them, 'Go and tell my brothers'. Once more, the central message of the Gospel is conveyed in a most unexpected way. It is these women who model faithful discipleship.

5 The guard at the tomb *Read Matthew 27:62–66; 28:11–15*

In contrast to the faithful ministry of the women, Matthew tells of the deceit of the Jewish authorities and the coercion of the Gentile soldiers who had been guarding the tomb of Jesus. This continues what we have already seen in earlier sections of Matthew's passion narrative: a strong tendency to blame the Jewish authorities for the death of Jesus. Now that Jesus is dead, these authorities are depicted as continuing their malevolent subterfuge. Matthew's polemic against the Jewish authorities continues to the very end of his Gospel.

The burial of Jesus, the discovery of his empty tomb, the early morning sighting of the risen Jesus by the women, and then the triumphant commissioning of the disciples atop the mountain by the glorified Lord: these happenings bring the story of Jesus to a marvellous and majestic conclusion. Yet, woven throughout this narrative is the account of the tawdry intrigue perpetuated by the Jewish leaders. Just as the resurrection of Jesus is becoming known, this group is attempting to keep this good news a secret. First they do this by means of armed force; but this fails when the earthquake comes, the angel rolls away the stone, and Jesus appears to the women. Then, the Jewish authorities engage in subterfuge, bribery and lies, in order to suppress the reports of the events that have taken place. This too fails when the risen Jesus appears to a wider group of his disciples. The truth will out, despite strenuous attempts to keep it bound.

Perhaps these curious scenes at the end of Matthew's Gospel serve as a timely reminder to us that faithful discipleship is costly. Just at the time when we expect the story to move into a grand, triumphalist key, Matthew tells this sobering tale. The disciples of Jesus are going to have to muster great courage if they are to proclaim, 'He is risen'. Their message will bring them into conflict with the Jewish and Roman authorities who have conspired to keep this news a secret. Discipleship will be difficult. It may well be that it can only be carried on when the final promise of Jesus is known as a reality: 'I am with you always, to the end of the age.'

6 The great commission *Read Matthew 28:16–20*

The women have already witnessed the risen Jesus. In this final scene of the Gospel, the eleven (male) disciples now come face to face with the transformed Jesus. The focus, however, is not on what had happened to Jesus in his transformation from crucified to risen; rather, it is on the task that now confronts his followers. These eleven disciples become representatives of all who follow Jesus. The charge they receive resonates in the ears of all who have followed Jesus since that time.

The words of Jesus in this closing scene provide another sample of Matthew's unique material. Jesus speaks of his global authority, echoing the claim he had made at 11:27. He now passes on that authority to his followers, for they are to take up the roles that he has exercised up to this point: making disciples, as Jesus has done (4:18–22; 8:18–22; 9:9), and teaching people, as Jesus also has done (5:1—7:29; 13:1–53).

Yet these words of Jesus offer a far-reaching commission that marks a new era in the story. Found nowhere else in the New Testament, his commands move the scope of the disciples' mission beyond anything that has happened in the story up to now. The resurrected Jesus tells the disciples to undertake a new type of mission that was never envisaged or foreshadowed in the rest of the Gospel. The words of Jesus at the end of the Gospel move beyond the prohibitions of the earlier mission (10:5—'Go nowhere among the Gentiles'). Now, the message of Jesus opens up to the world of the Gentiles in a way that is quite revolutionary.

The story of Jesus up to his arrest, as Matthew tells it, has been set almost entirely within the Jewish community. The activities of Jesus and his disciples have been confined to Israel. Beyond that story, however, the future surely now lies in a post-resurrection mission that opens up to the whole known world.

The mission that Jesus now commands has its source in his resurrected power. The disciples gather to worship the resurrected Jesus in much the same way as Christian communities gather each week to worship the resurrected Jesus. It is this reason for gathering that unites believers across the world. The Jewish renewal movement that Jesus began has truly become a worldwide movement of relevance to all peoples.

GUIDELINES

Throughout the history of the Christian Church, there has been a long-standing tradition at Easter of recalling and reflecting on Jesus' death and the events leading up to it. The death of Jesus by crucifixion is remembered each year in our services of worship on Good Friday. Likewise, Jesus' resurrection is celebrated on Easter Sunday. Both these events are central elements in the Christian faith, foundational to our understanding of how God's grace can be known.

Our study has ended with the Easter story, a story still well known among Christians and non-Christians alike. Even though many are familiar with the details of Jesus' suffering and death, they still do not know Jesus as a living force in their lives. How can we encourage those who waiver at the edge of faith to see beyond the apparent defeat of death on the cross to the triumph of resurrection? How do we convince others that the Jesus 'back then' is still available to us in the here and now?

One of the most important gifts of the resurrection was that of mission. Jesus in his earthly life was engaged in mission, having been sent into the world by God. At the end of Matthew's Gospel, Jesus commissions the disciples to carry on this mission, and bestows on them his authority. Resurrection carries not only the assurance of God's gift of eternal life, but also requires the mission of all believers.

Jesus was raised from the dead in order to ensure that the message of his resurrection, the power of God and the promise of new life is spread throughout the world. If we are to follow Jesus as his disciples, then we too, like the disciples of long ago, must go into our communities and spread the news about the love of God and the assurance of God's grace to all people. As the Church, Jesus charges us with this responsibility. Our response to the resurrection should not stop at believing. It also requires action.

Although the earthly Jesus has departed this world, we are given another gift of the resurrection, the Holy Spirit. We have in the Holy Spirit a guide, and a continuous presence that strengthens, enlivens, renews and sustains us. As resurrected Lord, Jesus fills us with the renewing power of the Spirit, and enables the mission of God to continue.

These words of Jesus assured and strengthened the first disciples as they faced the future with fear. May they likewise speak to us and assure and empower us so that we too might engage in the mission that was begun by Jesus, as renewed and revitalized people, who by our lifestyle reflect the resurrection life and faith.

For further reading

In addition to the works listed at the end of the notes in the previous two issues of *Guidelines*, see:

J. L. Houlden, *Backward Into Light. The Passion and Resurrection of Jesus According to Matthew and Mark*, SCM Press 1987

A. Le Grys, *Preaching to the Nations. The Origins of Mission in the Early Church*, SPCK 1998

Hosea

The first verse of the book of Hosea tells us that the prophet exercised his ministry from about 750BC. Hosea therefore appeared on the scene shortly after the prophet Amos and, like him, addressed his words to the northern kingdom, which he calls Israel or sometimes Ephraim. With the death of King Jeroboam II in about 747BC, a period of relative stability and prosperity (for some at least!) came to an end. The next twenty-five years were to see the rapid decline and fall of the northern kingdom. Internally there was turmoil, intrigue and political assassination. One pretender who seized the throne lasted only one month (2 Kings 15:8–15). Externally the threat from the Assyrian empire was growing. First they annexed Galilee and then destroyed what was left of the northern kingdom in 722BC, taking many people into exile.

Whether Hosea was still alive in 722BC to witness all this, we do not know. In fact, we know very little about him at all, and what we do know is confined to the prose portions in chapters 1 and 3. These tell of his marriage to a woman called Gomer and the birth of three children. The relationship between these two chapters and the time sequence involved is disputed. There are three options:

- *They both refer to the same incident and to the same woman, Gomer.*

- *They refer to two separate incidents but the woman is the same—Gomer left Hosea and he bought her back.*

- *They refer to two distinct incidents and two different women.*

Sometimes these two chapters dominate discussion of Hosea and there is a great temptation to try to psychoanalyse the prophet and draw all sorts of conclusions from his 'personal tragedy'. Such speculation is best avoided however. The image of the faithless wife does provide an important metaphor for God's relationship with the people of Israel, but Hosea uses many other images for God too. We should avoid reading the whole book solely through the lens of chapters 1 and 3.

Hosea's message was primarily aimed at the northern kingdom of Israel and its capital Samaria. His words of warning were unheeded, and Samaria was destroyed in 722BC. Hosea's words were not forgotten, however. Refugees fled to the southern kingdom of Judah, and it seems likely that Hosea's message was preserved there. It is possible that the words of Hosea were added to by the southern editors in order to make specific points relevant to a southern audience during the next century or so.

The Hebrew text of Hosea's poetry is often quite difficult and obscure. This may be because of poor copying of the text in the early days. Alternatively it may be that the text is correct but we do not understand it properly. Since Hosea was a northerner it may contain words or phrases in a northern dialect. This does mean that English translations vary quite markedly from one another in some verses. I shall base my own comments on the New Revised Standard Version.

16–22 APRIL   **HOSEA 2; 4–8**

1 Sex, lies and rewinding the tape *Read Hosea 2:2–23*

This chapter explores in poetic form the implications for Israel of the stories of Hosea's family life described in the narratives of chapters 1 and 3. The imagery in verses 2–5 is blatantly erotic, and its portrait of female sexuality is deeply unflattering. However, other prophets such as Jeremiah and Ezekiel pick up the image and take it even further.

The Bible portrays a constant battle between the ethical religion of Yahweh, the God of Israel, and the cult of Baal, the fertility god of the Canaanites. The God of Israel had his natural 'home' in the desert, especially at Mount Sinai, leading the people through the barren wilderness for forty years. In contrast, Baal was a god of fields and crops, who bestowed the life-giving rains. Once the Israelites stopped being wandering nomads and became settled farmers there was a strong temptation either to abandon worship of the Lord and turn to Baal, or to confuse the two and say Yahweh = Baal. Hence the prophetic insistence that it is the Lord who provides the staple crops of grain, wine and oil (v. 8). Canaanite practices also entered into the worship life of the nation, so the prophet announces that all religious festivals will cease (v. 11).

From verse 14 the mood changes as the deserted husband becomes the tender lover. A second courtship and marriage will take place. A series of reversals is portrayed as Israel experiences again the 'days of her youth' when the people came out of Egypt. The story of the Valley of Achor (meaning 'Trouble Valley') is told in Joshua 7. Second time around it will become instead a 'door of hope' (v. 15). There will no longer be any confusion between Yahweh and Baal (vv. 16–20). The term Baal is actually a title rather than a proper name. It means master, husband, lord, implying a sense of ownership. This title *baal* will no longer be used, but rather the term *ish* (meaning husband/man) which has a more tender, less proprietary ring to it.

In verses 21–23 the chapter returns to the names of the prophet's three children given in 1:4–9, Jezreel (the place of a notorious and bloody battle in 2 Kings 9), 'not pitied' and 'not my people'. Now the negative associations of these names will be removed. The name Jezreel literally means 'he sows' and the prophet plays on this name in verse 23. The place of battle and death will become a place of new growth. Similarly the daughters experience transformation—the Israelites will once more be the people of the Lord, enfolded in the arms of the compassionate God.

2 Standing in the dock *Read Hosea 4:1–19*

Chapter 4 opens with the language of the law court. We can perhaps imagine the prophet speaking in God's name and pointing an accusing finger at the guilty citizens gathered for a festival in Samaria or Bethel. First comes a general indictment of the people in verses 1–3. They have broken many of the fundamental rules of human behaviour, so that social cohesion is breaking down. Verse 2 in particular spells out evils that are contrary to the Ten Commandments. The sentence is passed in verse 3: the land and everything that lives on it will suffer the consequences.

In verses 4–8 the prophet turns his withering accusations

against the priests. As members of the religious establishment they had a responsibility to uphold the law of Moses, but they have failed in their duties. A decade earlier the prophet Amos had confronted the high priest of Bethel (Amos 7:10–14). Perhaps Hosea too faced hostility from the religious hierarchy because of his forthright preaching. The priests are no better than the people, the people no worse than the priests. So both will suffer the same fate (vv. 9–10).

Verses 11–14 focus on the worship life of the community. Again the Ten Commandments are being broken by the presence of wooden idols (v. 12). There are references elsewhere in scripture to the setting up of sacred wooden poles. These are called Asherah —the same name as one of the goddesses of the Canaanites. Many sanctuaries were situated on the tops of hills or near wells, springs or groves of trees (v. 13). The phrase 'under every green tree' was later to sum up the infiltration of illicit, extravagant and indecent customs into Israelite worship. Verse 14 suggests that the practice of religious prostitution may also be taking place. This is not just 'common' prostitution but officially sanctioned activity—and all in the name of organized religion.

Verses 15–19 sum up the sad state of affairs. The northern kingdom of Israel is corrupted and the southern kingdom of Judah is warned not to incur guilt. (Is this a sideways glance by Hosea to the situation over the border in his own day, or is it part of the work of the Judean editors addressing a southern audience?) The great sanctuaries of the kingdom are best avoided. Beth Awen (House of Evil) is Hosea's contemptuous name for Bethel (House of God). Very similar statements about Gilgal and Bethel were made by Amos (Amos 5:5).

3   The clouds of war   *Read Hosea 5:1–15*

The first seven verses of this passage continue the theme of faithlessness. Throughout this chapter the favourite term used for the northern kingdom is Ephraim. This was the name of one of the sons of Joseph, and the territory allotted to Ephraim occupied a central position in the hill country. Because of its dominance, the name of this single tribe could be used to stand for the whole of the northern kingdom—just as sometimes people speak of 'England' when they really mean all of the United Kingdom.

At verse 8 there is a change in focus which may give a clue to the historical situation lying behind this section. For the first time the judgment and destruction is associated explicitly with warfare. This is marked by the warning given by the blowing of the ram's horn and sounding the alarm in verse 8. After the death of Jeroboam II in 747BC, the political situation declined. The aggressive campaigns of the Assyrian king Tiglath-Pileser threatened the security of smaller states like Syria, Israel and Judah. By the mid-730s, Pekah, the king of Israel, had formed an alliance with Rezin, the Syrian king in Damascus. They sought to enlist Ahaz, the Judean king, in their alliance against the Assyrian menace. When he refused they waged war on him and tried to depose him. The background to this Syro-Ephraimite war against Judah can be found in Isaiah 7. It was the occasion on which the prophet Isaiah originally spoke his famous Immanuel prophecy. These upheavals of 735–733BC may lie behind verses 8–15. King Ahaz of Judah appealed for help to the king of Assyria, and the Syrian/Ephraimite alliance was defeated. Much of the northern kingdom was confiscated, so that only the territory of Ephraim itself was left independent. King Pekah was assassinated and a new king, Hoshea, sued for peace with the Assyrian king (v. 13)

It is worth noting how daring are the images of God which the prophet employs. The Lord is depicted as a wasting sickness and disease (vv. 12–13) and like a hungry young lion (v. 14). At exactly the time Isaiah was offering words of reassurance to the southern king that 'God is with us' (Immanuel), Hosea warns the north of the opposite. Verse 15 is about God's withdrawal from the scene. It is a theology not of presence but of absence.

4   True repentance?   Read Hosea 6:1–11

In verses 1–3 we hear an exhortation to return to the Lord for healing and restoration. Are these words composed by the prophet Hosea as a model for the people to say? Or do they reflect an actual liturgical piece from the dismal days of the 730s to 720s? Behind them lies an assumption that the Lord definitely will heal and restore. On the surface they are quite beautiful, with the Lord compared to the welcome dawn and the fruitful showers (v. 3). The reference to 'three days' in verse 2 was quoted by Church Fathers from the second century onwards as a prophetic pointer to the resurrection of Jesus.

Therefore, when quoted in isolation, or as a response to the warnings of chapter 5, these verses read well. However, when read alongside verses 4–6 they appear rather differently. Those verses emphasize the shallow and ephemeral nature of Israel's response to God. It is as fleeting as morning cloud, as easily dispersed as dew (v. 4). Though verses 1–3 use the language of 'turning', there is almost no recognition of genuine sin. Forgiveness is taken for granted. God will forgive because that is what God does! Perhaps the lesson of the passage is that forgiveness cannot be bought so cheaply—it is a costly thing.

Verse 4 onwards are words spoken by God. They portray God's exasperation and longing for the people of Israel. Even when the Lord sends them prophets they reject them (v. 5). Verse 6 is one of the most famous verses in Hosea, demanding mercy and faithfulness. Is this verse saying faithfulness *instead of* sacrifice, therefore repudiating the sacrificial system? Or does it mean faithfulness *more than* sacrifice, so that ritual may exist but only in second place? The verse is quoted by Jesus in Matthew 9:13 and 12:7.

Verses 7–10 give details of atrocities committed in the land. Some commentators think they refer to incidents from past history, perhaps from the time of Judges. Others think they refer to events in Hosea's own day—the details of which we cannot know for sure. Finally, the first half of verse 11 may be one of those additions by the southern editors of the book. Judah needs to beware too, or it will suffer the same fate as its sister kingdom. No room for complacency in Jerusalem, therefore.

5   Alliances and assassinations   *Read Hosea 7:1–16*

The dating of the oracles in this chapter can probably be fixed to the reign of the last king of Israel, King Hoshea, who reigned from about 732BC until just before the fall of Samaria in 722. Since the death of Jeroboam II, political instability had grown worse and worse. Of the next five kings no fewer than four were assassinated within the space of a dozen or so years (for details see 2 Kings 15:8–31). A setting in the early 730s seems to fit best the sayings in verses 3–7. Intrigue piles on intrigue as different factions vie for power. The image of the burning oven represents the 'overheated' state of politics in the north. Verse 7 sums it up: 'all the kings have fallen'.

The instability of the monarchy affected not only the internal affairs of the kingdom but was reflected in foreign policy too. A *coup d'état* often signalled a change in direction in foreign affairs. Some kings were willing to accept Assyrian dominance, while others fought against it. Thus King Menahem paid tribute to the Assyrian king (2 Kings 15:19–20) while King Pekah resisted and formed an alliance with the king of Damascus. This led to the Syro-Ephraimite war which ended in defeat for Israel and the loss of much of its territory (2 Kings 15:29). The last king, Hoshea, was initially placed on the throne by the Assyrians as a puppet ruler of what was left of the northern kingdom. He could not resist playing the political game, however, withholding tribute from Assyria and looking to Egypt for help (2 Kings 17:4). Hence the references to Egypt in verses 11 and 16.

We can now understand the reference to foreigners devouring the strength of Israel in verse 9. The nation is sick and ageing, drawing near to death. Like a senseless dove or pigeon it flits between Assyria and Egypt (v. 11). Even when they moan and wail in their distress, their actions are inappropriate (v. 14). They gash themselves in the kind of self-mutilation practised by the prophets of Baal on Mount Carmel seeking to rouse Baal to action (1 Kings 18:28). Is the Lord to be invoked as if he were Baal? Is this the kind of mourning he wants? Hosea has no doubt that the kingdom is approaching its nemesis.

6 Reaping the whirlwind   *Read Hosea 8:1–14*

The chapter begins with a summons to blow the trumpet. This may be God addressing the prophet to play the part of watchman, or a word of Hosea addressed to his audience. The covenant relationship is broken. The irony is, though, that the people do not recognize it. They think the 'special relationship' is still intact. They may think they know God, but they are deluded.

In the rest of the chapter Hosea goes on to specify just how and why the covenant has been broken:

- *Verse 4a: The king should be appointed by God, as the Lord's anointed one. From the start of its existence the northern kingdom had chosen its own kings, and lately one king followed another in swift succession. They are placed on the throne for reasons of political expediency or opportunism, they are not chosen by God.*

- *Verses 4b–6: Images were prohibited in the ten commandments. However, when the northern kingdom first split from the south, around 920BC, its first king, Jeroboam I, had set up bull images at the shrines of Bethel and Dan. Hence the mention of calf images in verses 5 and 6. They may refer to an image at the capital, Samaria, or to the ancient sanctuary at Bethel.*

- *Verses 7–10: Verse 7 consists of two short, pithy wisdom sayings. Actions bring consequences in their train, and so the nation will reap the whirlwind. Verses 8–10 return to the foolish-ness of the political process, especially in the dealings with Assyria. Here the image of seeking after lovers is associated with a flawed foreign policy, rather than false religious practices. However, the latter could often follow on the former.*

- *Verses 11–14: The religious life of the nation is once more in the spotlight. There is plenty of religion about—verses 11 and 13 indicate no shortage of sacrifices. Unfortunately there is precious little reverence for the commandments (v. 12) which really matter. In addition, the people rely on fortified buildings for protection rather than look to the Lord as their strong fortress and high tower.*

They have sown the wind—they will reap the whirlwind.

GUIDELINES

Here are some topics for prayer that arise from our reading of Hosea so far:

- *Pray for marriages under strain and for those agencies that seek to bring about reconciliation.*

- *Pray for all those—women, men and children—caught up in the trade of prostitution, both in your own country and around the world.*

- *Pray for nations where there is chronic political instability, whose people live with the threat of coup and violent revolution.*

- *Pray for yourself, that you may recognize and remove the false idols set up within your own life.*

23–29 APRIL   HOSEA 9—14

1 Lessons from history *Read Hosea 9:1–17*

We should perhaps imagine verses 1–6 spoken at a particular feast day (v. 5) at one of the great sanctuaries such as Bethel. The most likely setting is the autumn festival of Ingathering or Tabernacles, which was perhaps the most important of the pilgrimage feasts in Hosea's time. It celebrated the ingathering of the grapes and other summer fruit. It was a time of great rejoicing—but no more (v. 1). In this passage explicit references are made to exile and deportation from the land. Some Israelites will end up as refugees in Egypt, while others will be hauled off to the land of Assyria (v. 3). The city of Memphis (v. 6) was near the site of the pyramids and was renowned as a place of burials. How ironic that the descendants of the people who came out of Egypt in the time of Moses should now end their days back in the land of slavery.

Verses 7–8 are particularly intriguing, and most likely indicate some of the opposition Hosea had to face. It is very tempting to read these verses in the light of the story of Amos' experience as recorded in Amos 7:10–17. At the shrine of Bethel, Amos was challenged and sent packing by Amaziah the priest. Did history repeat itself in the ministry of Hosea? The prophet bemoans the fact that he is slandered as a fool and a madman. His answer is that he is merely fulfilling his calling to be a watchman (compare Ezekiel 33:1–9) and is continually harassed and derided for his pains.

From verse 9 onwards, and for several chapters to come, Hosea will allude to incidents from the history of Israel in order to highlight the nation's waywardness. Gibeah (v. 9) was the scene of a particularly notorious atrocity recorded in Judges 19–21. Baal Peor (v. 10) was a place just across the east side of the Jordan where, according to Numbers 25, the Israelites were seduced into the worship and immorality of the Baal cult. Gilgal (v. 15) was one of the first places in the Promised Land where the Israelites established a sanctuary after crossing the Jordan (Joshua 4). It was also the place where Saul was crowned king—thus fulfilling the people's desire to have an earthly ruler 'like other nations', and rejecting God as their true king (1 Samuel 8).

With a past like this and a dismal present there can be little hope for the future. Hence the repeated theme of these verses— no more children, and pity those who are conceived. We find an echo of this in Jesus' warning to the daughters of Jerusalem in Luke 23:28–29.

2   Down on the farm   *Read Hosea 10:1–15*

Throughout this chapter agricultural images are used to describe the situation of the people of Israel. First they are compared to a luxuriant vine (v. 1). This image was a popular one and is developed in particular in Psalm 80:8–13. Hosea's southern contemporary, Isaiah, extends the images in Isaiah 5:1–7, and Jesus tells a number of parables set in a vineyard (e.g. Mark 12:1–11; Matthew 20:1–16). Hosea declares that all the kingdom's prosperity has only led to ruin. The land is filled with rank weeds of wickedness (v. 4). In days to come the vineyard will be destroyed and thorns and thistles will grow in its sanctuaries (v. 8). Turning next to a farming image, Hosea pictures the people as a trained heifer ploughing the land. They are called upon to plough and sow in righteousness instead of evil (vv. 11–13).

Once again Hosea attacks the cultic establishment, especially the bull image of Bethel (vv. 5–8). Most significant in this chapter however is the sustained attack upon the monarchy as an institution. The biblical witness is ambivalent about the value of kings. There are passages which celebrate the royal line of David in particular. However, the compilers of 1 Samuel 8 were not so sure. The founding of the monarchy under Saul at Gibeah is seen as a failure of nerve, and evidence of a lack of trust in the Lord. This may be the sin of Gibeah mentioned by Hosea in verse 9, if it does not refer to the Judges 19–21 episode. Hosea apparently viewed the whole royal enterprise as a profound mistake. Here his prophecy differs from Isaiah, which contains a number of positive royal messianic pronouncements. In contrast this chapter sees the end of the line of northern kings. The people themselves will recognize their worthlessness (v. 3), the king will perish ignominiously (v. 7), defeated at the very start of the battle (v. 15).

The final sentence of verse 10 is directly quoted by Jesus in Luke 23:30 as he stops to speak to the women of Jerusalem. Luke's previous verse, 23:29, echoes the barrenness theme of Hosea 9. Therefore it would seem that this section of Hosea has played a significant part in the language of Luke's account of Jesus meeting the women as he carries his cross through the streets of Jerusalem.

3 Mother love   Read Hosea 11:1–11

This is one of the loveliest passages in the book of Hosea. Verse 1 is quoted in Matthew 2:15 as a prediction of the flight into Egypt by Mary and Joseph with the infant Jesus. In the context of Hosea's own preaching, however, it is plainly a reference to the Israelite exodus from Egypt, when the infant nation was described as God's first-born son (see Exodus 4:22). Having used the husband and wife image to great effect, Hosea now turns to that of parent and child.

Our first instinct may be to think of a father figure in this passage—especially in view of other biblical texts which speak of

Israel has become no better than a Canaanite—and a crooked one at that. Still, what would you expect with an ancestor as dubious as Jacob!

5 Final warning   *Read Hosea 13:1–16*

This chapter contains many themes that we have met before. They include the calf idols (v. 2), the transitoriness of the people (v. 3), the God of the exodus and the first commandment (v. 4), the divine shepherd (vv. 5–6) who becomes a ravening beast (vv. 7–8), the futility of kingship (vv. 9–11), the unwise son (vv. 12–13), and the end of Samaria (vv. 15–16). The overall impression is that this is perhaps the most threatening and gloomy analysis in the book—especially the daring image of God as a wild animal in verses 7–8.

It is possible that these words are among the latest in the book of Hosea, just prior to the final catastrophe in 722BC. The reference to Ephraim in verse 1 is to the specific tribe which once had such pre-eminence among the twelve tribes (Deuteronomy 33:13–17). Once others trembled before him, but now Ephraim is pitifully reduced. In the final days of the northern kingdom only a woefully small area centred on Samaria was left independent. Verse 10 could refer to the capture of King Hoshea by the invading armies before they went on to lay siege to Samaria (see the account in 2 Kings 17:1–6). The specific fate of the capital city amid the horrors of war is the theme of verses 15–16. The wind from the east (the direction of Assyria) was the hot desert wind which dried up everything before it.

So almost every verse in chapter 13 appears thoroughly negative and gloomy. What then is the tone of verse 14? The first half of the verse may be taken as questions expecting the answer 'No' ('Shall I redeem…?') followed by a summons to the powers of death to come and do their worst. This is how most modern translations interpret the sense, and the surrounding context would support that. On the other hand, since ancient Hebrew did not have the equivalent of a question mark, the words can be read as statements of intent ('I shall redeem…') followed by a challenge thrown down to the deadly powers. Most of the ancient versions, including the

Greek translation of the Bible known to the New Testament writers, follow this interpretation as do the AV and NIV in English (although the sense then requires that the last line of verse 14 be attached to verse 15). Not surprisingly, therefore, when the apostle Paul quotes the verse in Greek in 1 Corinthians 15:55, he understands it as a positive statement. He uses it in his argument for the powerlessness of death in the face of the resurrection.

6 Repentance and restoration   *Read Hosea 14:1–9*

The final chapter of Hosea ends the book on a note of exhortation and promise. It begins with a summons to return to the Lord, followed in verses 2–3 by a model prayer of repentance composed by the prophet for the people to learn. This genuine repentance is what they must offer, rather than the many vain sacrifices. The prayer includes a repudiation of both foreign alliances and idolatry.

In verses 4–7 God responds with a promise to renew his penitent people. The language here is exuberant and filled with images taken from nature. It is reminiscent of the kind of love poetry found in the Song of Songs. Indeed Hosea, more than any other writer in the Old Testament, stresses the love of God for his people.

We have seen how bold Hosea is when it comes to the use of metaphors for God. In verse 8 he produces an image found nowhere else in the Old Testament. He pictures God as a tall and shady evergreen tree, a tree of life to the people. Indeed throughout this chapter Hosea uses bold nature imagery to speak of God. He takes over the fertility language of the Canaanite religion in order to show that it is the Lord who is the source of new life and growth, and not the gods and goddesses of Canaan.

The book ends with a concluding comment in verse 9. This may be a late addition by an editor who wants to encourage the reader to meditate and reflect on the message of the book. It uses the language of wisdom writings, such as the book of Proverbs. It is a final indication that the words of Hosea spoken during the period 750–720BC were still being treasured long after. They have been preserved for us too, so that we can reflect upon their haunting message.

GUIDELINES

The book of Hosea is particularly rich in imagery and metaphor, applied both to God and to the people. Here are some of the positive images of God used in the latter part of the book. Choose one or more of these and quietly reflect on what they mean for you. Use your senses and imagination to the full.

God as nursing mother	*Hosea 11:3–4*
God as guiding shepherd	*Hosea 13:5*
God as tender healer	*Hosea 14:4*
God as refreshing dew	*Hosea 14:5*
God as shady tree	*Hosea 14:8*

Further reading

G.I. Davies, *Hosea, Old Testament Guides*, Sheffield Academic Press, 1993

G.I. Davies, Hosea, *New Century Bible Commentary*, Sheffield Academic Press, 1992

H. Mowvley, *The Books of Amos and Hosea*, Epworth Commentaries, Epworth Press, 1991

The Bible Reading Fellowship
Peter's Way, Sandy Lane West, Oxford, OX4 5HG
ISBN 1 84101 132 0

Distributed in Australia by:
Willow Connection, PO Box 288, Brookvale, NSW 2100.
Tel: 02 9948 3957; Fax: 02 9948 8153;
E-mail: info@willowconnection.com.au
Available also from all good Christian bookshops in Australia.
For individual and group subscriptions in Australia:
Mrs Rosemary Morrall, PO Box W35, Wanniassa, ACT 2903.

Distributed in New Zealand by:
Scripture Union Wholesale, PO Box 760, Wellington
Tel: 04 385 0421; Fax: 04 384 3990; E-mail: suwholesale@clear.net.nz

Distributed in South Africa by:
Struik Book Distributors, PO Box 193, Maitland 7405, Cape Town
Tel: 021 551 5900; Fax: 021 551 1124; E-mail: enquiries@struik.co.za

Distributed in the USA by:
The Bible Reading Fellowship, PO Box 380, Winter Park,
Florida 32790-0380
Tel: 407 628 4330 or 800 749 4331; Fax: 407 647 2406;
E-mail: brf@biblereading.org; Website: www.biblereading.org

Publications distributed to more than 60 countries

Printed in Denmark

BRF MINISTRY APPEAL RESPONSE FORM

Name _____

Address _____

_____ Postcode _____

Telephone _____ Email _____

(tick as appropriate)

Gift Aid Declaration

☐ I am a UK taxpayer. I want BRF to treat as Gift Aid Donations all donations I make from the date of this declaration until I notify you otherwise.

Signature _____ Date _____

☐ I would like to support BRF's ministry with a regular donation by standing order (please complete the Banker's Order below).

Standing Order – Banker's Order

To the Manager, Name of Bank/Building Society _____

Address _____

_____ Postcode _____

Sort Code _____ Account Name _____

Account No _____

Please pay Royal Bank of Scotland plc, London Drummonds Branch, 49 Charing Cross, London SW1A 2DX (Sort Code 16-00-38), for the account of BRF A/C No. 00774151

The sum of _____ pounds on ___/___/___ (insert date your standing order starts) and thereafter the same amount on the same day of each month until further notice.

Signature _____ Date _____

Single donation

☐ I enclose my cheque/credit card/Switch card details for a donation of
£5 £10 £25 £50 £100 £250 (other) £ _____ to support BRF's ministry

Credit/ Switch card no. ☐☐☐☐☐☐☐☐☐☐☐☐☐☐☐☐☐☐☐

Expires ☐☐ ☐☐ Issue no. of Switch card ☐☐☐

Signature _____ Date _____

(Where appropriate, on receipt of your donation, we will send you a Gift Aid form)

☐ Please send me information about making a bequest to BRF in my will.

Please detach and send this completed form to: Richard Fisher, Chief Executive, BRF, Peter's Way, Sandy Lane West, OXFORD OX4 6HG.
BRF is a Registered Charity (No.233280)

GUIDELINES SUBSCRIPTIONS

Please note our subscription rates 2001–2002. From the May 2001 issue, the new subscription rates will be:

Individual subscriptions covering 3 issues for under 5 copies, payable in advance (including postage and packing):

		UK	surface	airmail
GUIDELINES	each set of 3 p.a.	£10.50	£11.85	£14.10
GUIDELINES 3-year sub	i.e. 9 issues	£25.00	N/A	N/A

Group subscriptions covering 3 issues for 5 copies or more, sent to ONE address (post free):

GUIDELINES	£8.85	each set of 3 p.a.

Please note that the annual billing period for Group Subscriptions runs from 1 May to 30 April.

Copies of the notes may also be obtained from Christian bookshops:

GUIDELINES	£2.95 each copy

GUIDELINES SUBSCRIPTIONS

❏ I would like to give a gift subscription (please complete both name and address sections below)
❏ I would like to take out a subscription myself (complete name and address details only once)

This completed coupon should be sent with appropriate payment to BRF. Alternatively, please write to us quoting your name, address, the subscription you would like for either yourself or a friend (with their name and address), the start date and credit card number, expiry date and signature if paying by credit card.

Gift subscription name _____

Gift subscription address _____

_____ Postcode _____

Please send to the above, beginning with the January 2001 issue:

(please tick box)

	UK	SURFACE	AIR MAIL
GUIDELINES	❏ £10.50	❏ £11.85	❏ £14.10
GUIDELINES 3-year sub	❏ £25.00		

Please complete the payment details below and send your coupon, with appropriate payment to: **The Bible Reading Fellowship, Peter's Way, Sandy Lane West, Oxford OX4 6HG**

Your name _____

Your address _____

_____ Postcode _____

Total enclosed £ _____ (cheques should be made payable to 'BRF')

Payment by cheque ❏ postal order ❏ Visa ❏ Mastercard ❏ Switch ❏

Card number: ☐☐☐☐ ☐☐☐☐ ☐☐☐☐ ☐☐☐☐

Expiry date of card: ☐☐☐☐ Issue number (Switch): ☐☐☐☐

Signature (essential if paying by credit/Switch card) _____

NB: BRF notes are also available from your local Christian bookshop.

GL0101   The Bible Reading Fellowship is a Registered Charity

BIBLE READING RESOURCES PACK

A pack of resources and ideas to help to promote Bible reading in your church is available from BRF. The pack which will be of use at any time during the year includes sample editions of the notes, magazine articles, leaflets about BRF Bible reading resources and much more. Unless you specify the month in which you would like the pack sent, we will send it immediately on receipt of your order. We greatly appreciate your donations towards the cost of producing the pack (without them we would not be able to make the pack available) and we welcome your comments about the contents of the pack and your ideas for future ones.

This coupon should be sent to:

The Bible Reading Fellowship
Peter's Way
Sandy Lane West
Oxford OX4 6HG

Name _____

Address _____

_____

_____ Postcode _____

Please send me _____ Bible Reading Resources Pack(s)

Please send the pack now/ in_____ (month).

I enclose a donation for £_____ towards the cost of the pack.

BRF PUBLICATIONS ORDER FORM

Please ensure that you complete and send off both sides of this order form.
Please send me the following book(s):

		Quantity	Price	Total
Books for Lent				
189 4	Faith Odyssey (*R.A. Burridge*)	_____	£6.99	_____
123 1	The Road to Easter (*J. Gardner & C. Leonard*)	_____	£8.99	_____
024 3	When They Crucified My Lord (*Brother Ramon*)	_____	£6.99	_____
People's Bible Commentary				
030 8	PBC: 1 & 2 Samuel (*H. Mowvley*)	_____	£7.99	_____
118 5	PBC: 1 & 2 Kings (*S. Dawes*)	_____	£7.99	_____
070 7	PBC: Chronicles—Nehemiah (*M. Tunnicliffe*)	_____	£7.99	_____
031 6	PBC: Psalms 1—72 (*D. Coggan*)	_____	£7.99	_____
065 0	PBC: Psalms 73—150 (*D. Coggan*)	_____	£7.99	_____
071 5	PBC: Proverbs (*E. Mellor*)	_____	£7.99	_____
028 6	PBC: Nahum—Malachi (*G. Emmerson*)	_____	£7.99	_____
046 4	PBC: Mark (*D. France*)	_____	£7.99	_____
027 8	PBC: Luke (*H. Wansbrough*)	_____	£7.99	_____
029 4	PBC: John (*R.A. Burridge*)	_____	£7.99	_____
082 0	PBC: Romans (*J. Dunn*)	_____	£7.99	_____
3280 0	PBC: 1 Corinthians (*J. Murphy-O'Connor*)	_____	£7.99	_____
073 1	PBC: 2 Corinthians (*A. Besançon Spencer*)	_____	£7.99	_____
012 X	PBC: Galatians and 1 & 2 Thessalonians (*J. Fenton*)	_____	£7.99	_____
119 3	PBC: Timothy, Titus and Hebrews (*D. France*)	_____	£7.99	_____
092 8	PBC: James—Jude (*F. Moloney*)	_____	£7.99	_____
3297 5	PBC: Revelation (*M. Maxwell*)	_____	£7.99	_____
Other new books				
194 0	Taking Hold of Life (*M. Killingray*)	_____	£6.99	_____

Total cost of books £ _____

Postage and packing (see over) £ _____

TOTAL £ _____

See over for payment details. All prices are correct at time of going to press, are subject to the prevailing rate of VAT and may be subject to change without prior warning.
NB: All BRF titles are also available from your local Christian bookshop.

PAYMENT DETAILS

Please complete the payment details below and send with appropriate payment and completed order form to:

The Bible Reading Fellowship,
Peter's Way,
Sandy Lane West,
Oxford OX4 6HG

Name _____

Address _____

_____

_____ Postcode _____

Total enclosed £ _____ (cheques should be made payable to 'BRF')

Payment by cheque ❏ postal order ❏ Visa ❏ Mastercard ❏ Switch ❏

Card number: ☐☐☐☐☐ ☐☐☐☐☐ ☐☐☐☐☐ ☐☐☐☐

Expiry date of card: ☐☐☐☐ Issue number (Switch): ☐☐☐☐

Signature (essential if paying by credit/Switch card) _____

Alternative ways to order

Christian bookshops: All good Christian bookshops stock BRF publications. For your nearest stockist, please contact BRF.
Telephone: The BRF office is open between 09.15 and 17.00. To place your order, ring 01865 748227.
Fax: Ring 01865 773150.
Web: Visit www.brf.org.uk

POSTAGE AND PACKING CHARGES				
order value	UK	Europe	Surface	Air Mail
£7.00 & under	£1.25	£2.75	£3.50	£5.50
£7.01–£30.00	£2.25	£5.50	£7.50	£11.50
Over £30.00	free	prices on request		